Parallel Processing
in Cellular Arrays

C³ INDUSTRIAL CONTROL, COMPUTERS AND COMMUNICATIONS SERIES

Series Editor: **Professor Derek R. Wilson**
University of Westminster, England

3. Dataflow Architecture for Machine Control
   Bogdan Lent

4. RISC Systems
   Daniel Tabak

6. Linear Control Systems
   VOLUME 1 – ANALYSIS OF MULTIVARIABLE SYSTEMS
   T. Kaczorek

7. Linear Control Systems
   VOLUME 2 – SYNTHESIS OF MULTIVARIABLE SYSTEMS AND
   MULTIDIMENSIONAL SYSTEMS
   T. Kaczorek

8. Transputers in Real-Time Control
   Edited by **G. W. Irwin** *and* **P. J. Fleming**

9. Parallel Processing in Cellular Arrays
   Y. I. Fet

10. Direct Digital Control Systems
    J. B. Knowles

Parallel Processing in Cellular Arrays

Y. I. Fet
Russian Academy of Sciences, Novosibirsk

RESEARCH STUDIES PRESS LTD.
Taunton, Somerset, England

JOHN WILEY & SONS INC.
New York · Chichester · Toronto · Brisbane · Singapore

RESEARCH STUDIES PRESS LTD.
24 Belvedere Road, Taunton, Somerset, England TA1 1HD

Marketing and Distribution:

Australia and New Zealand:
Jacaranda Wiley Ltd.
GPO Box 859, Brisbane, Queensland 4001, Australia

Canada:
JOHN WILEY & SONS CANADA LIMITED
22 Worcester Road, Rexdale, Ontario, Canada

Europe, Africa, Middle East and Japan:
JOHN WILEY & SONS LIMITED
Baffins Lane, Chichester, West Sussex, England

North and South America:
JOHN WILEY & SONS INC.
605 Third Avenue, New York, NY 10158, USA

South East Asia:
JOHN WILEY & SONS (SEA) PTE LTD.
37 Jalan Pemimpin 05-04
Block B Union Industrial Building, Singapore 2057

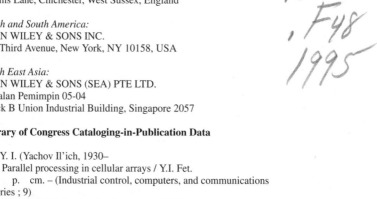

Library of Congress Cataloging-in-Publication Data

Fet, Y. I. (Yachov Il'ich, 1930–
    Parallel processing in cellular arrays / Y.I. Fet.
        p.   cm. – (Industrial control, computers, and communications
    series ; 9)
        Includes bibliographical references and index.
        ISBN 0-86380-164-1 (Research Studies Press). – ISBN 0-471-95409-8
    (Wiley)
        1. Parallel processing (Electronic computers)   2. Array
    processors.   I. Title.   II. Series.
    QA76.58.F48   1995
    004'.35—dc20   94–23056
                                                              CIP

British Library Cataloguing in Publication Data

A catalogue record for this book
is available from the British Library.

ISBN 0 86380 164 1 (Research Studies Press Ltd.)
ISBN 0 471 95409 8 (John Wiley & Sons Inc.)

Printed in Great Britain by SRP Ltd., Exeter

Contents

Preface   *viii*

Editorial Foreword   *ix*

Foreword   *xi*

Chapter 1   **Introduction: The Need for High-Performance Computing**   *1*

Chapter 2   **Parallel Computing**   *7*

Chapter 3   **Universal and Specialized Cellular Arrays: Distributed Functional Structures**   *18*

3.1.   Sequential and Parallel Automata   *18*

3.2.   Iterative Networks   *22*

3.3.   Parallel Substitution System   *24*

3.4.   Homogeneous Computing Media   *27*

3.5.   Distributed Functional Structures   *29*

3.5.1. *CAM as a Classical DF-Structure*   *31*

3.5.2. *Complex Associative Searches*   *36*

3.5.3. *Maximum Search (α-structure)*   *37*

3.5.4. *Minimum Search (β-structure)*   *40*

3.5.5. *Threshold Searches (ε-structure)*   *41*

3.5.6. *Between-The-Limits Searches (γ-structure)*   *43*

3.5.7. *Adjacency Searches (υ-structure)*   *44*

3.5.8. *Component-Wise Comparison (η-structure)*   *46*

3.5.9. *Classification (ρ-structure)*   *47*

3.5.10. *Compression (λ-structure)*   *48*

vi

Chapter 4   **Functional Possibilities of Distributed Functional Structures**   *51*

     4.1.   Analysis of α-structure   *51*

         4.1.1. *Matrix Memory Unit*   *51*

         4.1.2. *Homogeneous Computing Media*   *53*

         4.1.3. *Logical Functions*   *58*

         4.1.4. *Associative Memory*   *60*

         4.1.5. *Programmable Logic Array*   *63*

         4.1.6. *Functional Memory*   *64*

     4.2.   Analysis of λ-structure   *67*

         4.2.1. *Unitary Coding*   *67*

         4.2.2. *Digital Compressors*   *68*

         4.2.3. *Code Transformers*   *74*

         4.2.4. *Threshold Elements*   *78*

Chapter 5   **Solving Numerical Problems**   *80*

     5.1.   Binary Arithmetic Based on Vertical Processing   *80*

     5.2.   Table Look-Up Arithmetic Units   *83*

     5.3.   Arithmetic Computations in Unitary Codes   *89*

     5.4.   Arithmetic Units in Residue Number Systems   *91*

Chapter 6   **Non-Numerical Data Processing**   *104*

     6.1.   Features of Non-Numerical Problems   *104*

     6.2.   Database Machines   *104*

         6.2.1. *Classification of DBMs*   *106*

         6.2.2. *IDM-500*   *110*

         6.2.3. *Delta*   *111*

     6.3.   Labelled Array Method   *115*

     6.4.   Positional Sets   *120*

     6.5.   Combinatorial Memory   *124*

     6.6.   Modular Non-Numerical Computer   *127*

     6.7.   Set-Intersection Processor (ω-structure)   *129*

Chapter 7   **Interconnection Networks**   *131*

     7.1.   Introduction   *131*

     7.2.   Definitions   *132*

7.3.   Functional Possibilities of Interconnection Networks   *135*

7.4.   Kautz's Interconnection Network   *141*

7.5.   Sorting Networks   *143*

    7.5.1.   *Batcher's Sorting Network   144*

7.6.   Sorting in DF-structures   *147*

7.7.   Other Operations of Data Structure Transformation   *150*

    7.7.1.   *Flip Network   152*

7.8.   DF-structures as Interconnection Networks   *154*

    7.8.1.   *α-structure as a Connector   154*

    7.8.2.   *λ-structure as a Specialized Network   156*

Chapter 8   **Implementation of Cellular Microprocessors**   *159*

8.1.   Specialization   *159*

8.2.   Autonomus Instruments   *161*

    8.2.1.   *Robot Movement Control   162*

    8.2.2.   *Measurement and Sorting in Mass Production   162*

8.3.   Functional Modules   *163*

    8.3.1.   *Constructive Blocks of Computers   163*

    8.3.2.   *DF-structures in a Grid Massively*
                      Parallel Processor   164

    8.3.3.   *Economical Connector Based on λ-structure   167*

    8.3.4.   *Functional Computations in λ-structure   169*

8.4.   Combined Architectures

    8.4.1.   *The Basis of Combined Architecture   170*

    8.4.2.   *An Example: the Mixed Associative-Systolic*
                      Computer   172

    8.4.3.   *Heterogeneous Computing   173*

8.6.   VLSI Implementation of DF-structures   *176*

References   *179*

List of Acronyms   *183*

Author Index   *185*

Subject Index   *187*

Preface

by
Professor em.Dr.Dr.h.c.mult.**Wolfgang Händler**,
University of Erlangen-Nürnberg, Germany

Looking around it becomes evident: This world is working in parallel and with a multitude of elements of respective levels. Atoms cluster to molecules, molecules to fluid substances or to enzymes. Higher order substances are finally the basis of organic cells, which makes possible in general the <origin of life>. Between the elements of one respective level a multitude of simultaneous interactions take place which explain the behaviour and appearance of an entity. One special level of understanding organic life is the consideration of neural networks. Understanding parallel processing means in part to model computing in cellular arrays, i.e. in very simple rectangular and homogeneous matrix structures.

Yakov I. Fet describes in his book an interesting class of cellular arrays, Distributed Functional Structures. They possess very simple cells and intercell connections, implementing direct mapping of given algorithms into the circuits of specific logic nets. In designing new generation computers, these devices could present a particular type of building blocks, more flexible and intelligent than the common adders, multipliers, etc.

The reader will see that many known computations may be efficiently realized if they are embedded in corresponding "micro grained" functional structures. The author follows a line which was originally suggested by Yevreinov (1962).

Yakov I.Fet will lead the reader to a new comprehension of computation and at the same time to faster computing by bit-level parallel procedures. He develops and represents a wealth of his own ideas and the experience also of other sources. The book summarizes in a pragmatic way most of what is known in the area of computing in cellular arrays. At the same time the reader may become acquainted with a specific line of research in Russia, and particularly in Novosibirsk.

Editorial Foreword

by
Professor **Derek R. Wilson**,
University of Westminster, England

Shortly after the prime minister of the Russian Republic (then within the former USSR) - now President Yeltsin - was standing on a tank outside the Russian White House with the world watching and waiting for cataclysmic civil war, I passed through Moscow on my way to Novosibirsk. Academics are renowned for flexible travel arrangements and in this case the route to Novosibirsk involved 'hitching' a lift on a converted fighter bomber that was on a private flight for a certain aircraft factory in Novosibirsk - rather like arranging a day out at Blackpool courtesy of British Aerospace's Military Aircraft Factory at Warton. Such radical changes have taken place in Eastern Europe that the pace of the change is hard to comprehend. In former times you would have risked being shot for being outside the factory gates - let alone using the internal facilities for your own convenience. The reason for my visit was to speak at a conference on Parallel Computing organised by the Siberian Division of the Russian Academy of Sciences, and it was through Professor Fet's contribution that the idea of this monograph was born.

Parallel computing was an accepted practical computing technique in the former USSR long before its recent popularity in the 'West'. The Russian development of parallel computing methodology was in part driven by their poor technology. Computing speed was, in part, achieved by exploring parallelism through necessity, necessity in this case being the true Mother of Invention.

Professor Fet has made a creative and distinguished contribution to the subject, and this monograph presents a great deal of original work particularly in the area of Cellular Microprocessors. Professor Fet has presented a conceptual model of a practically universal set of functions that can be used to implement various arbitrary schemes for computing devices. It is through the conceptualisation of the computing design process that a universal computing medium can be conceived.

Professor Fet has written a book in the great tradition of Russian Academicians - a book that places emphasis on a rigorous theoretical underpinning to the subject, but which also considers the implementation. It is a great pleasure to welcome the book to this Series and to recommend it to you as an important exposition of the subject.

Foreword

Computers have become an integral part of our life. Their possibilities are rapidly increasing, and their size and cost are diminishing.

The most powerful supercomputers attain real performances of several billions of operations per second, in solving large scientific and engineering problems, and in the near future thousands of billions (teraflops) will be common. Non-expensive personal computers, in desk or portable version, are now indispensable tools for scientists, engineers, businessmen, students, and housewives.

At the same time, however, science, industry and commerce bring forward new large-scale problems, which cannot be solved by existing computing systems; the computing power of these systems must be increased by several orders.

The most realistic way to achieve this high performance will be to use of a multitude of processors in parallel computing systems. New approaches to parallelism have been researched by many universities and companies. These investigations involve all aspects of computer science, such as computing methods, algorithms, architecture, technology, and the desired result may be achieved only by a coordinated development.

The overwhelming majority of modern parallel computers, which are used for solving intensive computation problems, are based on a large number of concurrently working self-contained computing devices, such as microprocessors, transputers, and custom processors. These architectures have achieved significant results.

However, these systems have not yet utilized, with some rare exceptions, the latent reserves of *microparallelism*, that is, of simultaneous processing of all bits of initial data.

Many approaches can be used to organize the microstructure of computing devices, for instance, cellular automata, systolic arrays, programmable logic arrays, etc. One of these approaches, the *homogeneous computing media*, has been developed in Russia (especially in Novosibirsk) since the 60s. This is what lies behind the author's research presented in this book.

The book discusses *specialized distributed functional structures*, in which direct mapping of algorithms into schemes is accomplished; this means that algorithms of basic operations are modelled by specialized logic networks in the process of signal propagation. We call such functional devices *cellular microprocessors*.

In Chapter 1, basic problems involving the processing of huge amounts of data are briefly reviewed, in connection with the use of high-performance computers. Chapter 2 presents a short survey of parallel computing systems. Chapters 3 and 4 are devoted to the synthesis and analysis of Distributed Functional structures (DF-structures).

All problems encountered in computing systems are reducible, in principle, to three types of procedures in various combinations, which have their characteristic features and require, for their efficient implementation, specific approaches. These are: arithmetic processing, non-numerical processing, and data transfer and permutation. In Chapters 5, 6, and 7 it is shown how massive parallelism and other useful features of DF-structures can be utilized for realizing these types of procedures.

In the last, 8th, Chapter several examples are given showing applications of cellular microprocessors in computing systems.

Novosibirsk,   Yakov Fet
June 1994

CHAPTER 1

Introduction: The Need for High-Performance Computing

The need for a significant rise in computing power is recognized in virtually all fields of science and technology. There are, first of all, the problems which have been characterized by Kenneth Wilson [81] as "Grand challenge problems". The problems concerned are those of aerodynamics, nuclear technology, material science, weather prediction, molecular biology, modelling of economic systems, and others. Any considerable achievement in one of these challenging domains might be as influential on human life as the discovery of a new law of nature.

Supercomputers are of decisive importance in the development of these fields, as they accelerate theoretical research and reduce the costs of modelling and experimentation (e.g., aerodynamic testing), and sometimes they open new domains of investigation where experimentation is not possible (as in astronomy).

During the last decade, VLSI technology has enabled new computing methods and software to be developed, and the invention of new architectural concepts has led to a rapid expansion of computers and supercomputers. During this period the computing power of supercomputers has increased every three years by 2 or 3 times. In Table 1.1 are shown the main characteristics of some of renowned modern supercomputers. In the 90s we are expecting a new sharp rise in performance, probably by as much as 25 to 100 times [18].

Table 1.1. CHARACTERISTICS of MODERN SUPERCOMPUTERS

SYSTEM MODEL	MANUFAC- TURER	NUMBER OF PEs	PEACK PER- FORMANCE (GFLOPS)	MEMORY SIZE (GBYTE)
NCUBE 2S	NCUBE	8 - 8K	33 MFLOPS - 34 GFLOPS	UP TO 32
CRAY T3D	CRAY RESEARCH	32 - 2K	4 - 300	0.5 - 128
GS	PARSYTEC	64 - 16K	1 - 400	2 - 512 MBYTE
CM-5	THINKING MACHINES	32 - 16K	4 - 2000	UP TO 500
PARAGON XP/S	INTEL	32 - 4K	2 - 300	UP TO 128
VPP 500	SIEMENS/ NIXDORF	7 - 222	11 - 355	UP TO 55
CS-2	MEIKO	16 - 256	3 - 51	2 - 32

After all, the ultimate purpose of scientific and technological developments is the well-being of human society. The purposeful activity of man is directed at making objects and designing processes to satisfy, in ever-increasing measure, people's different needs, material as well as spiritual.

Technology plays a decisive role in material production. The purpose of modern production (with few exceptions that do not concern us here) is to provide people with high-quality and non-expensive food, clothes, dwelling, transportation, etc. To achieve this, one has to raise, throughout commerce and industry, efficiency, quality, flexibility, and reliability. This is possible only with broad application of modern computers and integrated automation.

For efficient functioning of a modern enterprise an integration of production is necessary, which presupposes unification by means of a common control system (based on computer networks), of all the functions required, such as designing, resource management, fabrication, assembling, testing, quality control, office work, etc. All subsystems of the future flexible manufacturing system must be connected by a communication network so that computers can work in all the subsystems, on all levels, making computer-integrated manufacturing [16] a reality.

In satisfying people's spiritual demands, computers are also indispensable, though in this field they are subordinate means.

People need information, so its creation, storage, propagation and consumption have to be organized. Radio, television, and the press are widely used means of propagation and consumption of information. At the same time, contemporary communications, particularly television and printing plants, use complex technological systems, involving various computing and control techniques.

Creation of new information is, of course, first of all the function of human natural intellect. But the role of technical tools is also essential. People of creative professions cannot do without modern libraries, telephones, personal computers, various databases, e-mail, etc.

A more and more important role in satisfying human needs will be played by various kinds of robot. Robots of the immediate future must possess not only motive functions, but also "organs of sense" (the corresponding research fields are computer vision, scene analysis and image processing, speech input and speech synthesis), and a "brain", allowing the robot to make independent decisions in complex dynamic situations (this is supported by intensive studies of artificial intelligence, including knowledge engineering, expert systems, neurocomputing, etc.).

Practically all problems treated by scientists or engineers are interrelated, to a considerable degree, with the application of mathematical methods and computations.

Mathematical problems of all kinds, arising in all domains of knowledge, may be reduced, in the end, to solving equations. These may be systems of finite equations, linear or non-linear; differential equations, ordinary or partial, with corresponding boundary value and initial data; integral and integro-differential equations; functional equations; etc. Only in simple cases will these equations allow exact solutions. In most cases an approximate numerical solution is needed, but this often creates a massive computational overload.

Classical methods of mathematics have not been oriented towards efficient computational procedures, but only at human abilities of computation. For complicated problems, no numerical results were attainable before the advent of computers. From that time on, the methods of applied, and even of pure, mathematics, have been deeply influenced by the capabilities of computing technique.

Mathematicians are trying to adapt their methods to the abilities of existing computing systems. This concerns, e.g., "vectorization" of problems, allowing us to solve them efficiently on vector-pipeline computers; development of parallel-pipeline versions of known numerical methods (such as those of linear algebra, or of signal processing) for high-speed computation in systolic arrays; designing of numerical algorithms with "prefix" operations fitting the structure of massively parallel systems.

On the other hand, in designing new computing system architectures, computer engineers try to take advantage of new developing mathematical methods. A good example of this is the Massively Parallel Processor [5] specially designed for high-performance processing of images received from satellites. The main architectural features of this system (rectangular processor matrix, nearest neighbour connections, computations with variable word length, etc.) are conditioned by the requirements of contemporary image-processing algorithms. In non-numerical processing, highly parallel database machines built on the relational data model are presently of particular importance.

In this process of correlated development of computing mathematics and computing technology the problem of *parallelizing* plays a special role. The fact is that, due to the physical restrictions of switching speed in the electronic elements, further increases in the performance of scalar and vector architectures become more and more troublesome. Thus, various kinds of parallel processing techniques have taken the foreground.

Some time ago, many mathematicians, under the burden of their specifically "human" experience of sequential organizing of computations, were rather sceptical about the possibilities of parallel implementation of algorithms. Fortunately, as shown by subsequent research, for most serious applied problems, mathematical approaches are possible, leading to regular data arrays and massive homogeneous computing procedures.

Parallel architectures of contemporary high-performance computing systems stimulate mathematicians to search for new ways of transforming algorithms in order to use to full extent the resources of hardware. Parallelizing is usually applied at the level of problems or problem fragments (*large-grain parallelism*), or at the level of data elements (*fine-grain parallelism*). Further increase in performance may be achieved by extending the principles of parallel processing to the level of single bits of argument arrays. On this last level, which we call *micro-grain parallelism*, we focus attention in this book.

Another important way of enhancing performance is *specialization* of hardware.

In solving any problem, the initial data and algorithms used have their particular features. In specialized computers, in contrast to general purpose computers, these features may be taken into account and used to achieve maximal efficiency. The best results are obtained, perhaps, when the architecture of the processor corresponds to the structure of processed data, and to the specific features of algorithms. For a large class of modern problems, the data are organized in two-dimensional bit arrays (numerical vectors and matrices, tables of characters, relations of relational databases, etc.). This determines the choice of two-dimensional distributed circuits as the basic structure of the processors considered in this book.

The features of algorithms, depending on specific problems, may be the order and rules of processing separate pieces of initial data, the way of forming final results from intermediate ones, etc. Thorough inspection of these features for a particular problem, or a class of problems, ensures the best mapping of the algorithm into the structure of a specialized net implementing it.

Last, the emphasis on homogeneity adopted here is of significant advantage for the designing and manufacturing of computers, as homogeneous structures perfectly fit to the topology and properties of modern VLSI.

With the development of parallel computing systems, the demands on their performance are constantly rising. Discussing the history of parallel processing, Wolfgang Haendler [33] compares it with the evolution of natural organisms. However, we may expect that, having achieved some level in his natural evolution, Man should be able to speed up the evolution of computers, using, in particular, the amazing abilities of computers themselves.

It is remarkable that Daniel Hillis, the designer of one of the most powerful and original computing systems, the Connection Machine, demonstrated in [43] the efficiency of using computers for optimization of computer architecture by means of genetic algorithms. Later on, Hillis wrote in [45]: "Perhaps, some future version of the Connection Machines will use circuits designed by these evolutionary methods".

CHAPTER 2

Parallel Computing

The idea of parallel computation arose long before modern computers. As early as in one of the papers of Charles Babbage we find a remark that if we had several arithmetic units, then the computer would be several times faster [32].

In 1949 Leonid Kantorovich, a noted Russian mathematician and economist, Nobel laureate, practically used what we would now call a "multiprocessing system" of a large number of punched card tabulating machines for simultaneous computation of tables of Bessel functions for all integer values of indices from 0 to 120 [20].

In 1958 Steven Unger suggested a project of a parallel computing system for pattern recognition [79]. This system contained a set of simple logical modules, Processing Elements (PEs), forming a rectangular array. Each module was connected with its eight nearest neighbours. All the modules implemented a common program, distributed by the main control unit. Now we would call the Unger system a SIMD-system, or MPP System[*).

In 1962 Daniel Slotnick proposed another parallel computing system called SOLOMON (Simultaneous Operation Linked Ordinal MOdular Network) [73]. This system, as well as Unger's, had a common control unit and a

----

[*) Recently, the term *MPP* has been widely adopted as an abbreviation of "Massively Parallel *Processing*". It should not be confused with the name "MPP" of the famous Batcher's supercomputer, "Massively Parallel *Processor*" (see below).

matrix of 32x32 identical processing elements. The system used interconnections with the four nearest neighbours, the so-called NEWS-grid (for North, East, West, South). The interface with auxiliary memory was via peripheral PEs. Each PE had a single-bit arithmetic unit and a local memory of 4k bits. In contrast to the Unger system, a mechanism controlling the activity of the PEs was introduced into the project SOLOMON, which essentially enlarged the flexibility of programming.

The SOLOMON project was not realized. Apparently it emerged too early, when the technology was not mature enough for building such a system. Successfully working parallel computers, essentially following the idea of SOLOMON, appeared only in the 80s: DAP (Distributed Array Processor) [66] and MPP (Massively Parallel Processor) [5].

Also in 1962, Edward Yevreinov in Russia suggested the concept of *Universal parallel Computing Systems with programmable structure (UCS)* [83]. The main principles of UCS were:
- the basic element of UCS is a general purpose computer (Elementary Machine, EM);
- the UCS has a homogeneous structure, that is, it consists of identical, equally connected EMs;
- the number of EMs in the system can be changed;
- the instruction set, memory size and word length of an EM can also be changed.

It was also proposed to distinguish the UCSs:
- according to their topology: one-, two-, and multi-dimensional;
- according to the type of exchange between EMs: parallel, sequential, and parallel-sequential;
- according to the spatial arrangement of EMs: concentrated and distributed.

In the Yevreinov concept two levels of organization of parallel computing systems were considered: the *macrostructural*, which has just been briefly described, and the *microstructural*, concerning the inner structure of the elementary machines. Here a homogeneous approach was again proposed, based on so called *Homogeneous Computing Media* (HCM).

The main properties of the HCM are:

- homogeneity;
- short-range interaction;
- universality of the cells;
- possibility of setting each cell to implement any function from the chosen universal set.

According to Yevreinov, the HCM should be manufactured in a single technological process, like some "computing tissue", getting the required "pattern" at the last stage of production, by means of appropriate configuring.

Now we can recognize that, as early as the 60s, Yevreinov foresaw trends of development and the potentialities of future VLSI.

In our view, the ideas of Slotnick and Yevreinov anticipated by far the present state of computer science and outlined most of the fundamental problems of development of high-performance computing systems.

As was pointed out, Slotnick was not able to implement the SOLOMON system. However, he implemented successfully another of his projects of parallel computing systems. That was the celebrated ILLIAC IV, the first large-scale multiprocessor system [3].

ILLIAC IV contained 64 64-bit arithmetic units integrated into a rectangular lattice and working under the general control of the Burroughs 6700 computer. This system was working at the Ames Research Center of NASA from 1972 to 1983, and played an important role in the development and application of parallel algorithms and structures.

Many research projects and industrial developments of parallel systems arose in the 60s and the 70s. Thus, it became necessary to systematize and classify such systems.

In 1966, Michael Flynn introduced his famous classification [27]. He proposed to consider four types of system, according to dependence on the interaction of data and instruction flows:

* SISD - Single Instruction stream, Single Data stream;
* SIMD - Single Instruction stream, Multiple Data stream;
* MISD - Multiple Instruction stream, Single Data stream;
* MIMD - Multiple Instruction stream, Multiple Data stream.

This classification became popular and has been widely adopted up to the present time. However, the Flynns classification does not reflect some of the essential properties of modern computing systems, which leads sometimes to misunderstandings.

Wolfgang Haendler introduced in 1974 an interesting classification scheme [34], covering many of the important features of parallel computing systems. This is so-called Erlangen Classification Scheme (ECS).

This scheme is based on the "Erlangen triplet", defined as $t = (k,d,w)$, where k is the number of control units (CU), d is the number of arithmetic-logical units (ALU), w the word length. For instance, a 32-bit computer of von Neumann architecture is described, according to the ECS, by the triplet:

$$t_{von\ Neum.} = (1,1,32).$$

To describe more complicated architectures, the ECS provides three operations, allowing different compositions of structures:

$+$ for description of systems containing several different structures;

$*$ for description of systems with sequentially ordered (pipelined) structures;

$\vee$ for indication of alternative variants of using the same structure.

Thus, the ILLIAC IV may be described by the formula:

$$t_{ILLIAC\ IV} = (1,1,48)\ *\ (1,1,64),$$

where the first term corresponds to the machine B 6700, and the second to the matrix of PEs. To reflect the possible operation mode of processing half-words, the formula

$$t_{ILLIAC\ IV} = (1,1,48)\ *\ (1,64,64)\ \vee\ (1,128,32)$$

may be written.

To describe parallel-pipelined architecture, the Erlangen triplet is enlarged as follows:

$$t = (k*k',\ d*d',\ w*w'),$$

where k' is the number of CUs, interpreting the program jobs (the length of the macropipeline), d' the number of ALUs controlled by a single CU, and processing one data stream, w' the number of stages (segments) of the arithmetic pipeline.

Thus, the ASC computer of Texas Instruments, having four 8-segment arithmetic pipelines, is characterized by the formula:

$$t_{ASC} = (1,4,64*8).$$

The classification scheme of Haendler allows us to lucidly describe nearly any architecture by means of simple triplets and their combinations.

Using a large number of concurrently working computers (microprocessors) is presently the only way to achieve the necessary high performance. Different approaches are known to the problem of organizing the cooperative work of many computing devices: vector/pipeline architectures, parallel MIMD or SIMD architectures, dataflow computing, networking of workstations, etc. A voluminous literature is devoted to the analysis of these approaches and the description of various systems (see, for instance, [4, 19, 39, 46, 59, 68, 77]). We discuss here only the parallel architecture.

In the description and design of parallel computing systems, the notion *granularity* is often used. Granularity is a characteristic of the construction and functional possibilities of the processing elements.

A system is called *large-grained* if some computer or microprocessor (for instance, a standard 32-bit one) is used as a PE. *Fine-grained* systems are distinguished by comparative simplicity of PEs, that is, simplicity of construction and restricted functional possibilities. Processing elements of fine-grained systems are usually realized as customized integrated circuits.

As examples of large-grained parallel systems, the following may be cited:

- The above-mentioned SIMD-system ILLIAC IV, with 64-bit customized PEs.

- The MIMD system iPSC/2. It may contain up to 128 PEs, based on Intel 80386 32-bit microprocessors connected as a hypercube.

- The NCUBE/10 which is also a hypercube MIMD-system, containing up to 1024 PEs, implemented as customized VLSI chips (32- and 64-bit floating-point arithmetic).

Among various existing parallel architectures we will particularly distinguish the fine-grained SIMD structures with bit-sequential processing, having single-bit PEs, each connected by means of a one-bit bus with its local memory. The advantages of these structures are due to the fact that the coordinated work of a very large number of PEs (tens and hundreds of thousands) allows us to reach a super-high performance, in spite of the quite moderate performance of the separate PEs. The lower requirements to the PEs makes it possible to use simpler technology, and thus to decrease the costs. Hence, the fine-grained SIMD structures have a relatively high performance/cost ratio.

A classical example of such architecture is the STARAN system [67]. The supercomputers MPP, DAP, CM-1 and CM-2 [78] belong to the same category. In contrast to conventional computers, these systems use as operands *bit slices* (columns) of the arrays processed, instead of *words* (rows). Therefore they may be called *Vertical Processing Systems* (VPS) [35].

The important features of the VPS are the structure and throughput of the interconnection network used for communications between the PEs because these features are often the decisive factor influencing the system performance. The STARAN system exploits a specific *FLIP* network, which is a dedicated multistage network implementing a broad set of "butterfly"-type permutations and batch shifts. In the DAP and MPP only four nearest-neighbour connections are provided, forming a NEWS network.

In the BLITZEN project [9], which represents a development of Batcher's MPP designed especially for VLSI implementation, the PEs form a so-called X-grid, a two-dimensional network with interconnections in eight compass directions: N, NE, E, SE, S, SW, W, NW.

The CM-2 system has highly sophisticated interconnection means. These are, first, the NEWS grid, and, second, the hypercube interconnection network designed as follows. The 16 PEs on each custom chip are connected by a crossbar switch. 4096 (2^{12}) of such chips are placed in the vertices of a 12-dimensional cube comprising the 64K PEs of the full configuration. The message transfer between arbitrary two processors requires to pass at most 12 intermediate vertices. Thus, the PEs of STARAN make up a linear (one-dimensional) structure, PEs of DAP and MPP two-dimensional structures, and of CM a multi-dimensional one.

During the last decade, the VPSs have been generally recognized. Table 2.1 shows the main characteristics of some of contemporary VPSs.

According to the Haendler classification, for VPSs the following formulas can be written:

$$t_{STARAN} = (1, 8192, 1),$$
$$t_{DAP-610} = (1, 4096, 1),$$
$$t_{MPP} = (1, 16384, 1).$$

These formulas reflect some important features of vertical processing: unified control, massive parallelism, use of single-bit ALUs. However, they do not take into account such characteristics as topology and bandwidth of the interconnection network, capacity of local memory, organization and bandwidth of I/O channels.

To describe the topology of the VPS, one can introduce into the Erlangen Classification Scheme an additional sign (for instance, ":"). Then the formulas would take the form:

$$t_{STARAN} = (1, 1:8192, 1),$$
$$t_{DAP-610} = (1, 64:64, 1),$$
$$t_{MPP} = (1, 128:128, 1).$$

For various reasons, VPSs are of particular interest to us. First of all, these systems achieve the highest level of parallelism. Secondly, the structure of massively parallel systems is well correlated with

Table 2.1. CHARACTERISTICS of VPSs

SYSTEM MODEL	MANUFAC- TURER	NUMBER OF PEs	INTERCON. NETWORK	LOCAL MEMORY KBIT	MEMORY SIZE MBYTE
DAP-510	ACTIVE MEMORY TECHN.	1024 (32X32)	NEWS AND BROAD- CAST LINES	32	4
DAP-610	- - " - -	4096 (64X64)	- - " - -	64	32
MPP	LORAL DEFENCE SYSTEMS	16384 (128X128)	NEWS	1	2
CM-1	THINKING MACHINES CORP.	65536	HYPERCUBE	4	32
CM-2	- - " - -	65536	HYPERCUBE AND NEWS	64	512
STARAN	GOODYEAR AEROSPACE CORP.	UP TO 8192	FLIP	9	UP TO 10
BLITZEN	MICROEL. CENTER, NORTH CAROLINA	16384 (128X128)	X-GRID (EIGHT DI- RECTIONS)	1	2
GAPP	MARTIN MARIETTA EL. SYST.	10000- -82944	NEWS	128 BIT	1296 KBIT

the structure of the data and algorithms involved in many important problems: solution of algebraic and differential equations, simulation of physical phenomena by finite difference methods, processing of signals and pictures, etc. VPSs are best suited for various kinds of non-numerical processing, to which the basic problems of artificial intelligence are reduced. Hence, they are very promising in supporting the newest directions of development of computing systems.

The VPSs gave a powerful impetus to the development of *data parallel programming* paradigm. The source of this paradigm is in the very nature of problems to be solved. Actually, the overwhelming majority of complex and voluminous problems deal with data organized into large blocks (arrays) of homogeneous structure. In such highly parallel computers as VPSs, it is possible to assign an individual PE to each data element of the given array. This leads to the conception of *parallel variables* which are the variables spread among the processors of the system.

To ensure efficient work with parallel variables, a set of powerful and clever *parallel software primitives* was developed including *global, spreading, routing, scanning* operations, and others. It was shown (see, e.g. [8, 10]) that the parallel primitives of these families are fundamental to many algorithms of numerical analysis, mathematical physics, computational geometry, graph theory, etc.

Last, there are close relations between vertical computing systems and homogeneous distributed structures. One of the early papers of Daniel Hillis was just entitled "The Connection Machine: a Computer Architecture Based on Cellular Automata" [44]. The real Connection Machine is, in fact, used in statistical modelling of spatially distributed physical phenomena by the cellular automata technique. The same machine, however, turned out surprisingly efficient in parallel realization of most of the common methods of data processing, and has become one of the most powerful supercomputers.

In subsequent Chapters we intend to trace some relations between VPSs and Distributed Functional structures (DF-structures), the main concern of this book. It will be shown, for instance, that the joint use of VPSs and specialized homogeneous processors, in particular, of

16

DF-structures, in so-called Combined Architectures (see Chapter 8) allows to unmask the potential reserves of the vertical systems and to give the user a possibility of flexible changing of the style of programming.

The correlation between distributed, horizontal and vertical modes of processing is made clear by the conception of compression and extension of logic circuits. The schematic view of a distributed structure is shown in Fig.2.1.a. It represents a superposition of a

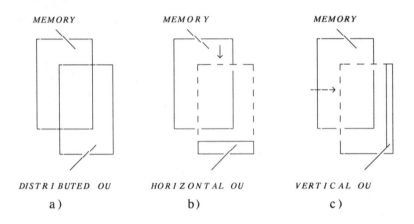

MEMORY   MEMORY   MEMORY

DISTRIBUTED OU   HORIZONTAL OU   VERTICAL OU

a)   b)   c)

Fig.2.1. Space-Time transformations.

two-dimensional logical network (a specific Operational Unit, OU) onto a two-dimensional memory unit which implements the given processing *in space*. Now, imagine that the memory is separated from the distributed OU, and then the latter is compressed in the vertical direction. Thus, we get the conventional horizontal (word-sequential) processing scheme with horizontal memory access (Figure 2.1.b). If the OU is compressed in horizontal direction, we get the vertical, bit-slice-sequential (*in time*), processing scheme with vertical memory access (Figure 2.1.c). Space-Time transformations of this kind were introduced by Hennie [40].

Thus, vertical processing represents a happy compromise. On the one hand, the vertical OUs are quite within the reach of the present technology; on the other hand, they ensure parallel processing of sufficiently large fragments of argument arrays. For example, if an array of 2^{14} 32-bit words has to be processed and the parallelism of the vertical OU is equal to 2^{14}, the whole processing requires only 32 time steps, i.e. it can be accomplished 2^9 times faster compared to the horizontal approach.

18

CHAPTER 3

Universal and Specialized Cellular Arrays: Distributed Functional Structures

3.1. Sequential and Parallel Automata

Description of all systems for digital information processing is based on the notion of the digital automaton. The digital automaton is a device transforming words into words. Fig 3.1 shows a scheme of an automaton with n inputs and m outputs. Assume the input and output alphabets are binary. Then the inputs may receive any of 2^n different binary words. When some input word w_{in} comes in, the automaton outputs the corresponding output word w_{out} of the set of 2^m possible combinations. The mapping $F: w_{in} \to w_{out}$ defined for all input words describes the rules of functioning of the automaton and, thus, the function it implements.

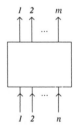

Fig.3.1. Digital automaton.

The automaton of the type just considered is called *finite automaton without memory*, or combinational circuit, the notion *finite* being related to the finiteness of input and output alphabets.

More complicated (and more powerful) automata are those *with internal memory.* The contents of this memory at any moment, or cycle, t define the *internal state* $s(t)$ of the automaton. The output word produced by the automaton depends now not only on the input word, but also on the internal state. At the end of each cycle, a new internal state $s(t+1)$ is produced, depending on w_{in} and $s(t)$. Thus, the function of the automaton with memory is described by mapping:

$$F: w_{in}, s(t) \rightarrow w_{out}, s(t+1).$$

All devices for digital information processing, including even the most complicated modern supercomputers, reduce eventually to the two models of finite automata discussed above. More accurately, each of these devices is a complex of appropriately connected automata.

Note that virtually all circuits of modern computers use binary alphabets (binary coding). Therefore these circuits are described, designed and studied by means of classical Boolean algebra, largely developed specifically for the needs of computer engineering.

Now consider a particular and very important example of an automaton with memory, the full binary adder (Fig.3.2). Inputs of the adder receive two one-bit binary summands, a and b, and the carry c from the preceding digit. At the outputs, the values of the sum s and the carry c' into the next digit are produced. The correspondence between the input and output combinations of binary variables is defined by the rules of binary addition, shown in Fig 3.2.b (the addition *truth table*). This table should be implemented by the combinational circuit of the adder CC. As it is known, the adder can be described, for instance, by the following logical functions:

$$s = ab\bar{c} \lor a\bar{b}c \lor \bar{a}bc \lor abc \quad \text{(the sum)},$$
$$c' = ab \lor ac \lor bc \quad \text{(the carry)}.$$

The flip-flop FF (a single bit of the internal memory) stores the carry c' (the internal state) and outputs it onto the input c at the next cycle.

20

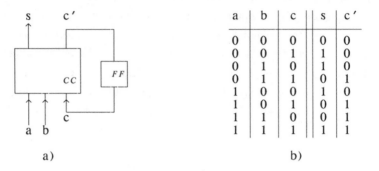

	a	b	c	s	c'
	0	0	0	0	0
	0	0	1	1	0
	0	1	0	1	0
	0	1	1	0	1
	1	0	0	1	0
	1	0	1	0	1
	1	1	0	0	1
	1	1	1	1	1

a)   b)

Fig.3.2. Sequential binary adder: a) general structure;
b) truth table of binary addition.

Fig.3.3 shows combinational logic circuits realizing the functions
s and c' in the basis AND, OR, NOT.

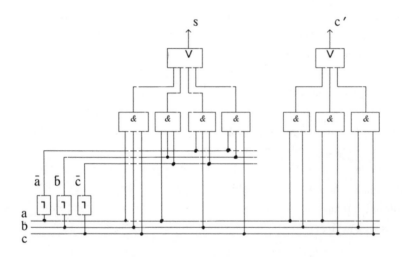

Fig.3.3. Implementation of sum and carry functions.

We have described the *sequential binary adder*. To sum two n-bit
binary numbers A and B by means of this adder, one has to feed
their bits (beginning with the least significant) into the inputs a
and b in the form of two time sequences:

$$A = a(t_1), a(t_2), \ldots, a(t_n) \qquad \text{and}$$

$$B = b(t_1), b(t_2), \ldots, b(t_n).$$

Then, the time sequence $S = s(t_1), s(t_2), \ldots, s(t_n)$ will correspond to the sum of A and B.

In principle, all possible computations can be performed by means of this simple device, the sequential adder, but very slowly.

The first obvious step to speed up the computations is to use n identical full binary adders. Fig.3.4 shows the corresponding circuit diagram of an n-bit *parallel binary adder*. Each digit has exactly the same circuit as the sequential adder of Fig.3.2, but the output of the carry in each position is connected to the input of the carry of the next digit. Now, when numbers $A = a_1 a_2 \ldots a_n$ and $B = b_1 b_2 \ldots b_n$ are fed into the inputs a_i and b_i, the sum $S = s_1 s_2 \ldots s_n$ is produced at the outputs s_i.

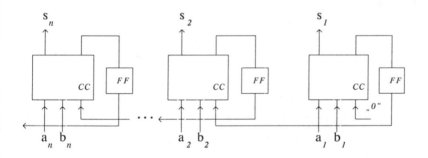

Fig.3.4. Parallel binary adder.

Of course, the carries should proceed sequentially through the chain of digits from the lower-order to the higher-order digit, and a lot of methods have been devised to speed up this run. But, in principle, this adder is a *parallel* adder, which can ensure a nearly linear (i.e. proportional to n) speed-up of addition, as compared to the *sequential* adder; naturally, at the expense of a large hardware cost: n single-digit circuits, apart from the pyramidal carry speed-up circuit.

At the very beginning of computer science, two models of computing device (automata) were introduced, the Turing machine, which was the model of sequential computing, and the von Neumann machine*, the model of parallel computing. We shall not consider these in detail, restricting ourselves to some brief remarks.

1. Both models are, of course, complete; that is, they allow realization of all computable functions.

2. The classical Turing machine model allows only sequential computation (like the finite automaton of Fig. 3.2.a).

3. The parallel von Neumann model is of special interest for our purpose, as a means to high performance. This model has several different interpretations. Two of these (iterative circuits and cellular automata) are considered next.

3.2. Iterative Networks

This model was studied in detail by Hennie [41].

An iterative network is a logical circuit consisting of identical and identically connected elements. Each element (cell) of an iterative network is a finite automaton (with internal memory, or combinational). In Fig.3.5 two examples of iterative networks are shown: one-dimensional (Fig.3.5.a) and two-dimensional (Fig.3.5.b). The inputs and the outputs of the cells are divided into intra-cell and outer. The intra-cell connections are represented by horizontal and vertical lines, the outer ones by oblique lines. The outer inputs are used to feed the independent variables. At outer outputs the results are produced. The intra-cell inputs and outputs belonging to the border cells of the network are called *boundary*. Sets of constants are usually fed to the boundary inputs, defining the mode of operation.

All inputs and outputs of the cells are usually considered to be binary.

----

* Not to be confused with von Neumann general purpose computer.

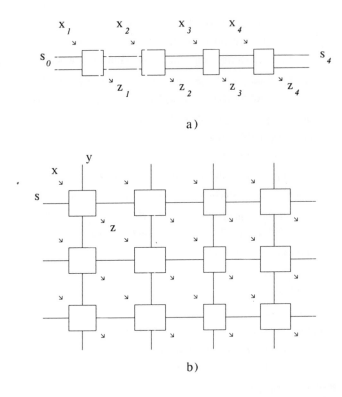

a)

b)

Fig.3.5. Iterative networks: a) one-dimensional;
b) two-dimensional.

The iterative network shown in Fig.3.5.a is a "chain" of cells having two channels of intra-cell connections. Such a network is called *one-dimensional two-channel*, with one direction of signal propagation (from left to right). Fig.3.5.b shows a *two-dimensional* network (a lattice) with two directions of signal propagation (from left to right and from top to bottom), one channel for each direction.

It is known [41] that any one-dimensional combinational iterative network with one direction of signal propagation is equivalent, in the sense of the transformation performed, to some finite automaton. This means that, to a *temporal* sequence of input signals $x(t_1)$, $x(t_2)$,... fed during the ordinary cycles into the inputs of the automaton, there corresponds a *spatial* sequence of input signals x_1, x_2,... fed concurrently to the 1-st, 2-nd,... cells of the iterative network. To changes of internal states of the finite automaton at transition from the preceding cycle to the next one correspond changes of intra-cell signals at their propagation from the preceding cell of the network to the next one; to the initial state correspond the signals at the boundary inputs; to the temporal sequence of output signals corresponds the spatial sequence of output signals of the appropriate cells of the network.

Construction of an iterative network corresponding to a given finite automaton is called by Hennie *time-space* transformation. In this transformation, to the time coordinate describing the data processing in the automaton is related the spatial coordinate describing the processing in the iterative network.

It is natural also to consider also an inverse *space-time* transformation (see Chapter 2), which specifies a finite automaton corresponding to a given iterative network.

Hennie's model is used later on in this Chapter in designing various specialized homogeneous functional structures.

3.3. Parallel Substitution System

This system [2] deals with so-called *cellular spaces*, that is, sets of identical cells (automata). To each cell, at each moment (cycle), two values are related: the *number* m of the cell, identifying the cell (constant for each cell), and the state a of the cell, a variable essentially expressing the data while processed. A finite set of cells forms a *word*, or a *configuration* (if the space representation of the automaton is meant). Fig 3.6 shows a simple pattern of three cells. Clearly, it can run through eight different states (configurations) in binary alphabet.

Data processing in this system is specified by listing the *substitutions* corresponding to the chosen algorithm. We demonstrate now the technique described in the example of summing an array of binary numbers, that is, reductive summation.

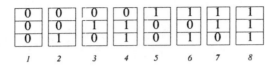

0	0	0	0	1	1	1	1
0	0	1	1	0	0	1	1
0	1	0	1	0	1	0	1

1   2   3   4   5   6   7   8

Fig.3.6. Configurations of cellular space.

Suppose five numbers have to be summed: 54, 21, 56, 29 and 26. Fig.3.7.a shows a matrix containing binary representations of these numbers. The algorithm of reductive summation contains just two substitutions (Figs 3.7.b and 3.7.c).

These substitutions are *parallel*, in the sense that each can be applied simultaneously to all configurations present at the given step in the cellular space that coincide with the left part of the substitutions describing the algorithm.

00110110 (54)
00010101 (21)
00111000 (56)
00011101 (29)
00011010 (26)

$$\begin{bmatrix} 1 \\ 01 \\ 00 \end{bmatrix} \longrightarrow \begin{bmatrix} 0 \\ 10 \end{bmatrix} \qquad \begin{bmatrix} 0 \\ 1 \\ 0 \end{bmatrix} \longrightarrow \begin{bmatrix} 1 \\ 0 \end{bmatrix}$$

a)   b)   c)

Fig.3.7. Reductive summation: a) argument array;
b) and c), substitutions of addition
algorithm.

Fig 3.8 illustrates the work of this algorithm. The presence of configurations allowing implementation of the first or the second substitution is marked by frames. Thus, at the first step the cellular space contains one configuration, corresponding to the left part of the first substitution, and four corresponding to the left part of the second. After applying corresponding substitutions the pattern changes, and at the second step three configurations arise for the first substitution, and three for the second. At the 10th step (in the present case) the process is finished, and the sum of the five

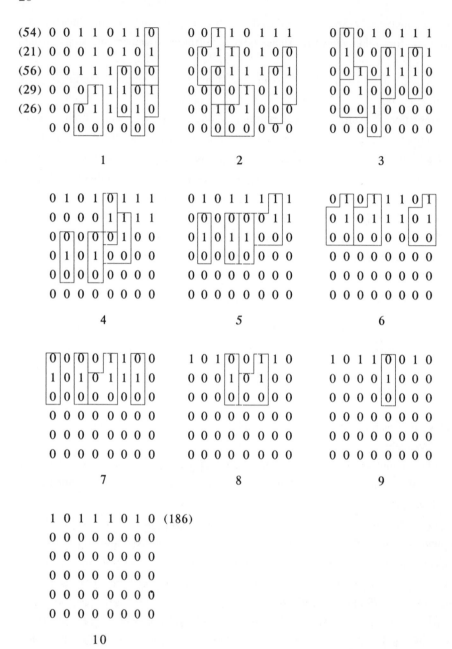

Fig.3.8. Ten steps of parallel addition in cellular space.

given numbers (186) is produced in the upper row of the matrix. Of course, for other specific summands a different number of steps would be needed.

As we see, this system is quite similar to the popular cellular game "Life", but nevertheless it can perform very useful task, computations. And, in the parallel mode, that is with high speed. Moreover, it has been proved that the parallel substitution system is *algorithmically complete*. Hence, it can perform *any* data processing.

Toffoly and Margolus discussed in [76] a family of Cellular Automata Machines developed at MIT. In each cellular machine, implemented as a plug-in board to a personal computer, a universal cellular space has been realized, as well as means of controlling its dynamics. It has much larger possibilities that the "Life" game. Each cell can take up to 16 states. By means of special tables the user can define rather complicated neighbourhoods and transition rules. Together with the graphic abilities of the host-computer, this provides a convenient means for studying and modelling the physics of continuous media, and many other important problems.

3.4. Homogeneous Computing Media

This interesting concept was introduced, as mentioned above, in 1962 by Yevreinov.

The cellular space is filled, as before, with identical elements, cells of a *homogeneous medium*. Usually square cells are considered, each connected with the four nearest neighbours.

The square form of the element is essential from the viewpoint of complete utilization of the chip area in modern planar integrated circuit technology. However, the cells should not necessarily be square. As is known, a dense filling of the plane is feasible also by other figures, triangles and hexagons.

The cell should be a *universal one,* i.e. it should be configurable to the implementation of all elementary logical functions of some complete basis (for instance, {AND,OR,NOT}), memory element function, interconnection functions, ensuring construction of arbitrary graphs from accordingly configured cell chains.

The theory of automata allows us to construct a logical net implementing an automaton in a given basis of logical elements, for any finite automaton, the functioning of which is described in some

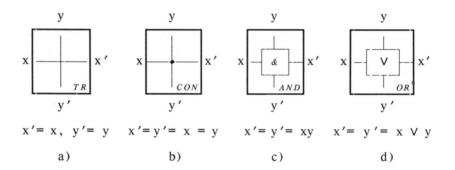

$$x' = x, \quad y' = y \qquad x' = y' = x = y \qquad x' = y' = xy \qquad x' = y' = x \lor y$$

$$a) \qquad\qquad b) \qquad\qquad c) \qquad\qquad d)$$

Fig.3.9. Four states of the universal cell of homogeneous medium.

specification language (e.g., by means of truth tables, as in Fig. 3.2.b). Moreover, various methods of minimization of logical nets according to definite criteria have been designed and implemented.

The main idea of homogeneous media is *embedding* of logical nets, that is, realization of arbitrary automata, into a planar homogeneous structure, by means of a corresponding configuration of cells.

Consider, for example, the implementation of the combinational circuit of the carry function of a full adder (Fig.3.3) in a homogeneous medium. In this case, it is sufficient to have cells with four states:

- interconnection element "transfer", TR (Fig.3.9.a);
- interconnection element "connection", CON (Fig.3.9.b);
- functional element AND (Fig.3.9.c);
- functional element OR (Fig.3.9.d).

Fig.3.10 shows one of the possible embeddings of the carry circuit into a section of a homogeneous medium of size 7 x 5.

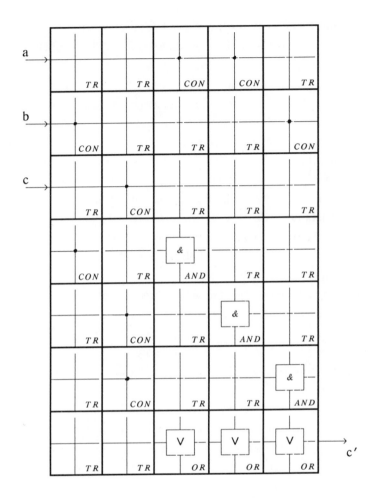

Fig.3.10. Embedding of carry function into homogeneous medium: $c' = ab \lor ac \lor bc$.

3.5. Distributed Functional Structures

We have considered several examples of homogeneous cellular automata. These devices are characterized by their high performance due to the extremely high degree of parallelism; that is, all bits of the data array are involved in concurrent processing.

The cellular automata machine cited above is used primarily for the investigation of processes in continuous media, by modelling those in cellular spaces.

Currently, many companies are trying to find ways of using the concept of cellular automata for designing general purpose computers. For instance, Digital Equipment Corporation proposed a Programmable Active Memory, PAM [7]. PAM is a rectangular mesh of identical cells called Programmable Active Bits, PABs. Each PAB is connected with four neighbouring PABs, and implements logical functions defined by a truth table loaded into the control register of this PAB. In the Paris Research Laboratory of DEC a universal reconfigurable homogeneous co-processor Perle-0 was built, representing a PAM of 3200 (40x80) PABs realized on the basis of Logic Cell Arrays (LCA) from Xilinx Inc. The reconfiguration of Perle-0 is accomplished by means of downloading the corresponding program by the host-computer into the control registers of the PAM. As reported, some complicated problems like high-accuracy multiplication, data compression, and image processing were solved in Perle-0 with one order of magnitude speed-up.

A similar approach is used by Algotronix Ltd. [13], Cellware Ltd. [61], and others.

Each of the models described is *universal* in the sense that it can realize arbitrary functions and algorithms, and the synthesis of necessary logical structures is accomplished by means of classical techniques of automata theory, such as transition tables, parallel substitutions, etc. [15].

When particular special functions are implemented by universal methods, significant redundancy is often observed. Thus, in the circuit of Fig. 3.10 only six of the total of 35 cells are really executing logical functions, that is, are processing. The other 30, equally valuable, cells play only a passive role of wires and connections.

One may ask whether it is possible, however, to use a homogeneous field of processing elements (cells) to obtain a more immediate implementation of given functions, bypassing classical ways, for instance, by means of simulation of processing, as is done in analogue computational devices. Perhaps, such simulation might ensure even higher performance and complete utilization of the chip area.

This kind of simulation is possible, at least for some important particular types of processing. In this book we shall consider mainly those *specialized* homogeneous structures which implement immediate mapping of algorithms into circuits. This means that in any such structure the given algorithm is simulated in the process of propagation of signals through the specialized logical net.

We call such schemes *Distributed Functional Structures* (DF-structures) [26]. A DF-structure is usually a rectangular matrix of binary memory elements superposed with a homogeneous combinational circuit (two-dimensional iterative array) implementing the given algorithm.

3.5.1. *CAM as a Classical DF-structure*

The classical example of a DF-structure is the Content-Addressed (associative) Memory (CAM), invented as early as 1956 by Slade and MacMahon [71].

A DF-structure realizing CAM functions is shown in Fig. 3.11. It is a rectangular matrix of dimensions m x n (Fig.3.11.a). Each cell (Fig.3.11.b) has one bit of memory and a logical circuit implementing the equivalence function:

$$s' = s(ca \lor \bar{c}\bar{a}). \qquad (3.1)$$

In addition, in each column of the matrix there is a bus c_j traversing all cells of this column, carrying the corresponding bit of the associative tag from the external *comparand register*.

This circuit acts as follows.

The binary signal s runs in the horizontal direction from left to right. If a boundary constant $s_0 = 1$ is applied to the input s of the leftmost cell of the row, then the values of the horizontal intra-cell signals depend on the relation of variables x and c. In accordance with (3.1), s = 1 is retained till a ≡ c. In that

32

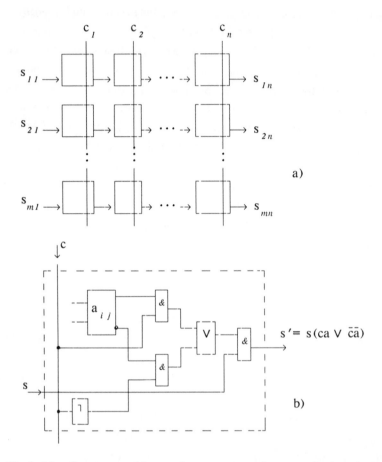

Fig.3.11. Content-addressed memory: a) general structure; b) logic circuit of an associative cell.

element where for the first time $x \neq y$, $s' = 0$ is produced, and this value of the signal s cannot change till it reaches the right boundary. If a binary word C (a comparand) is applied to the inputs c of the upper boundary, and the constants 1 are applied to the inputs s of the left boundary, then clearly the array will realize the functions of a CAM, that is, it will produce the *response* signal in the row (or several rows) containing the word (or words) which coincide with the given comparand C. Fig.3.12 shows an example of implementing an associative search. It represents a matrix of size 6x4 in which   six 4-bit words are written,   forming the argument array. The second argument of this procedure is a scalar, an associative tag, written in the comparand register. After accomplishing the associative search procedure, in the present case at the right boundary of the matrix, the third and the sixth rows coinciding with the comparand will be marked by "ones".

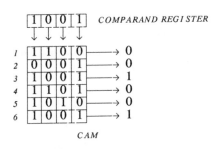

Fig.3.12. Example of associative search.

If the argument array and the comparand are written beforehand in the corresponding memory elements, then after the boundary signals $s_0 = 1$ are applied, and when the transition processes are finished, the results arise on the right boundary of the matrix. Thus, the algorithm of associative search may be considered to be modelled by the two-dimensional logical net of this scheme (Fig.3.11). This kind of modelling might be called *quasi-analogue simulation.*

The invention of associative memory was an important event in the history of computing. It was the first homogeneous device realizing parallel distributed data processing. At that time there were already homogeneous devices for other computer functions. First of all, these were *commutators*, adopted from telephony (the problems of commutation in computing systems are considered in some detail in Chapter 7). Then came *memory devices*, which had from the beginning a homogeneous distributed structure corresponding to the exact nature of the data stored. After the advent of content-addressed memories, the principle of homogeneous distributed processing began to penetrate into the third area, *operational devices*. Storing and processing are joint in

CAM. Therefore, such devices were called "logic-in-memory" or "active memory" devices.

As to the functional possibilities of the CAM, this operational device seems, at first sight, rather narrowly specialized, having equality search as the basic procedure. But really this is not true. Soon after the invention of the CAM, various authors suggested techniques of parallel implementation of different computational algorithms by this device.

Massive parallel computations in associative memories can be implemented by means of the method of consecutive transformation of the memory element states, introduced in 1963 by Fuller and Estrin [29]. This method will be illustrated by the example of massive addition.

Let $\underline{A}$ and $\underline{B}$ be numeric vectors to be summed component-wise. In the associative matrix three fields are specified: the field A for vector $\underline{A}$, B for vector $\underline{B}$, and C for carries. The width of the fields A and B corresponds to the word length of the summands (m); the field C consists of one column. The data are arranged so that each row contains components of the same name.

The addition begins with the least significant (right-hand) bits and proceeds through m cycles. In the first cycle the first bits of fields A and B are interrogated, as well as the column C (before beginning the process, column C should be cleaned). All the other bits of fields A and B are masked. The interrogation is carried out in accordance with the table of binary addition (Fig. 3.13). If all the rows containing combinations 000, 001,... in the analyzed positions are singled out in turn, and the corresponding values of functions s and c′ are written in those rows, addition of the first bits of all pairs of components will be accomplished. This procedure takes only 16 microinstructions (8 interrogations and 8 write operations), independently of the dimension of the vector summands $\underline{A}$ and $\underline{B}$.

Moreover, if the bits of the sums are written instead of those of the arguments (for instance, into field B), and the new carries instead of the previous (into column C), then the number of microinstructions in the addition cycle would decrease. Indeed, as seen from the table in Fig.3.13, in four cases out of eight (these

	a	b	c	s	c′
1	0	0	0	0	0
2	0	0	1	1	0
3	0	1	0	1	0
4	0	1	1	0	1
5	1	0	0	1	0
6	1	0	1	0	1
7	1	1	0	0	1
8	1	1	1	1	1

Fig.3.13.Parallel add i t i on in associative memory.

are underlined in the table), the values of the functions s and $c′$ coincide with the values of the arguments b and c, and thus the result is obtained at once. So, the transformations are needed only in the four other cases, and the cycle now contains only 8 microinstructions instead of 16 (4 interrogations and 4 write operations).

Thus, the method of consecutive transformations of memory element states allows implementation of massive addition for $8m$ steps (where m is the word length of the summands), independently of the dimension of the argument vectors.

Other massive parallel computations may be implemented by associative memory in a similar way.

Moreover, the basic operation of associative memory, the equality search, underlies the efficient solution of important data processing problems, such as the problems of data retrieval systems, free text search, database management, etc. (cf. Chapter 6). Recently the search operation has taken on special significance, because of the development of logic programming, expert systems, and other conceptions and techniques of artificial intelligence.

One might ask why content-addressed memories and associative parallel processors have not until now been broadly utilized. The main reason is the relative complexity of CAM cells. In spite of the striking achievements of VLSI technology, manufacturing of distributed associative memories of large enough size for practical applications remains a very serious problem.

Another, rather important, reason is that of human psychology. Foster, one of the leading specialists in associative architectures, wrote about this [28] that the conservatism of programmers, their wish to retain their hard-earned and highly valuable skill, prevents them from appreciating new computer architectures.

Nevertheless, the idea of parallel computations in the memory has continuously progressed, though in another technological version, the so-called *vertical* or *quasi-associative* parallel processors (STARAN, DAP, MPP, CM). We would like to note that these architectures developed from the conceptions of cellular automata, distributed processing, and associative memories, have now taken a leading position in the supercomputer market.

3.5.2. *Complex Associative Searches*

Now, we consider several other DF-structures implementing more complex data processing functions.

Classical associative memories are oriented towards the operation of *equality search*. Other kinds of search and comparisons (see below) are also used in practice.

Arguments of each of the search operations are a data array, with binary words (rows) as elements, and one or two special binary code combinations defining the search qualifications. The result of the search operation is some subset of the set of elements (rows) of the original array containing all elements satisfying the given qualification.

The search is fulfilled usually not over the whole array element, but over a definite field called an *associative tag*. Other fields have to be masked.

The main search operations are:

1. *Equality search.* Some code combination X is given, called the *comparand*. The result is the set of all elements with the associative tags A_i coinciding with the comparand.

2. *Inequality search.* The same as in the previous case, but the result is the set of all elements with tags A_i not coinciding with the comparand.

3. *Between-the-limits searches (searches in given intervals).* The comparands X_u and X_l are given, corresponding to the upper and lower bounds of the interval. The result is the set of all elements with the tags A_i satisfying one of the following inequalities:

$$X_l < A_i < X_u$$
$$X_l < A_i \leq X_u$$
$$X_l \leq A_i < X_u$$
$$X_l < A_i \leq X_u$$

4. *Threshold searches.* Some code combination T is given, called the *threshold.* The result is the set of all elements with tags A_i corresponding to one of the following relations:

$A_i > T$ Greater-Than Search (GTS),

$A_i < T$ Less-Than Search (LTS),

$A_i \geq T$ Greater-Than-or-Equal Search (GTES),

$A_i \leq T$ Less-Than-or-Equal Search (LTES).

5. *Adjacency searches.* A comparand X is given. The tags and the comparand are considered as binary numbers. The result of the search is the element with the tag A_i for which the difference $(X - A_i)$ is minimal.

This operation has two variants: *search of the nearest greater* and *search of the nearest smaller.*

6. *Searches of extremal values*:

the maximum search: $A_k = \max \{ A_i \}$;

the minimum search: $A_k = \min \{ A_i \}$.

We describe now DF-structures implementing directly complex associative searches [26].

3.5.3. *Maximum Search (α-structure)*

Consider a two-dimensional homogeneous structure of size n x m (Fig.

38

3.14.a), with m-bit elements of the processed array written in its memory so that each element occupies one row of the matrix (most significant digits to the left).

For the maximum search a known algorithm of bit-wise comparison of all elements is used, described as follows.

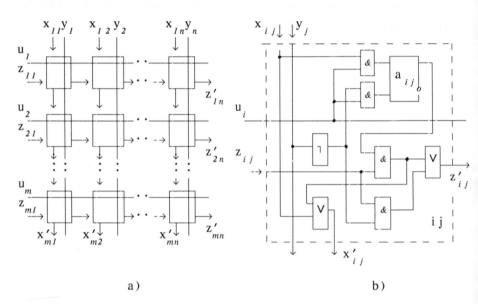

a)

b)

Fig.3.14. Maximum search: a) general structure of α-matrix; b) logic circuit of an α-cell.

Step 1. The contents of the first (left) column are looked over, that is, the most significant digits of all n elements. If all these digits are zeros, then at the following step the second digits of all n elements are looked over. If, however, the first column contains both zeros and ones, then at the second step only those elements which had ones in the first position are looked over.

Step j. The contents of the j-th column (j-th digits of all elements) are looked over, in those rows which were singled out at the (j-1)-th step. If all these digits are zeros, then at the following step the (j+1)-th digits of the same rows are looked over. If there are both zeros and ones in the memory elements looked over at the j-th step, then at the (j+1)-th step only rows corresponding to ones are looked over.

The subset of the rows singled out at the last (n-th) step (and this may consist of only one row) contains the maximal elements.

Now we show how the algorithm just described can be realized by means of a two-dimensional iterative circuit with two directions of signal propagation.

In the horizontal direction, it is necessary to have a chain looking over the contents of the memory elements sequentially from left to right and continuing this process if the current memory element contains one, or if all the memory elements in the analyzed column are zeros. This task can be done by a binary logic channel implementing in each cell of the iterative circuit the function:

$$z' = z(a \lor y),$$

where z' is the signal at the lateral output of the cell; z is the signal at the lateral input; a is the contents of the memory element; y is a variable characterizing the contents of the analyzed cells of the current column, so that $y = 0$ if all of them are zeros, and $y = 1$ otherwise.

Apply to the inputs z of all cells of the left column the boundary constants $z_0 = 1$. Then the presence of the signal $z' = 1$ in the horizontal channel of some row means that this row should be analyzed further; otherwise the signal z' takes the value zero, which cannot change later on.

Last, we must organize in each column a vertical chain checking the contents of all analyzed cells and producing the variable y. This can be done by means of a binary channel realizing in each cell the function

$$x' = x \lor az,$$

where x' is the signal at the bottom output of the cell; x is the signal at the upper input.

Apply to the inputs x of all cells of the upper row the boundary constants $x_0 = 0$. Then the intracell signal x' will take the value 1 in the first (from the top) of the cells which have to be analyzed (i.e. with $z = 1$) and contain one (i.e. with $a = 1$); the value $x' = 1$ thus obtained cannot change later on. Only when the analyzed column has no such cells does the vertical channel keep $x' = 0$, and the output of the lower (m-th) cell of the column $x'_m = 0$ is produced. For the proper functioning of the horizontal channels the value $y = 1$ has to be sent to all cells of such a column. Therefore, an additional vertical channel (bus) y should be organized, and its input in each column should be connected to the output x'_m.

Thus, the whole system of logical functions of a cell of the iterative circuit realizing the maximum search is as follows:

$$z' = z(a \lor \overline{y}), \qquad (3.2)$$
$$x' = x \lor az, \qquad (3.3)$$
$$y' = y, \qquad (3.4)$$
$$y_0 = x'_m. \qquad (3.5)$$

After the boundary signals $z_0 = 1$, $x_0 = 0$ are applied, and when the transition processes are finished, the signals $z' = 1$ at the right boundary of the matrix will appear in those rows which contain maximal elements.

Fig.3.14.b shows the functional scheme of an α-cell of the DF-structure we have considered.

3.5.4. Minimum Search (β-structure)

A structure for minimum search can be designed in a similar way. To single out the minimal elements by means of parallel bit-wise comparison, it is necessary, during the process of analyzing the rows, to continue the process if the memory element contains zero, or if all the memory elements analyzed in the current column contain ones.

These functions can be implemented by the same iterative circuit which was designed for maximum search, if the negations of the variables stored in the corresponding memory elements are used. Then the system of logical functions takes the form:

$$z' = z(\bar{a} \lor \bar{y}),$$
$$x' = x \lor \bar{a}z,$$
$$y' = y,$$
$$y_0 = x'_m.$$

3.5.5. Threshold Searches (ε-structure)

The ε-processor (Fig.3.15) has to single out all the elements A_i of the array A such that $A_i\theta$ T, where $\theta \in \{ =,\neq,>,\geq,<,\leq \}$.

For the synthesis of the DF-structure implementing this basic operation, the following algorithm is used.

In each row of the matrix A (simultaneously in all rows) is performed a bit-wise comparison of the number $A = a_{i1}a_{i2}...a_{in}$ stored in the memory elements of the cells of this row with the comparand $T = t_1t_2...t_n$. The interrogation begins from the most significant digits. Clearly, for any digit three situations are possible: a= t, a< t, a> t. If in the whole row no inequality is met, then $A_i = T$; if the first inequality met is $a_{ij} < t_j$, then $A_i < $ T, independently of the further comparison, as all further (less significant) digits have lesser weights; similarly, if the first inequality met is $a_{ij} > t_j$, then $A_i > $ T.

We now show that this algorithm can be implemented by means of a two-dimensional iterative network, each cell of which performs the logical functions:

$$z' = z(a \lor \bar{t}),$$
$$v' = v \lor z\bar{a}t,$$
$$t' = t,$$

where z, z', v, v', respectively, are input and output signals of horizontal channels z and v, a is the contents of the memory element, and t and t' are the input and output signals of the vertical bus t feeding the corresponding digit of the comparand T to the current column.

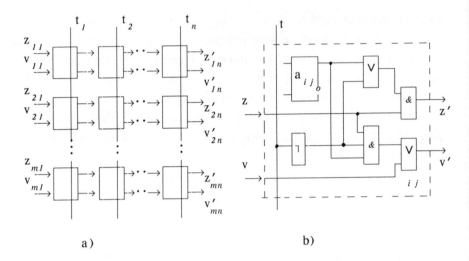

a)
b)

Fig.3.15. Threshold searches: a) general structure of ε-matrix;
b) logic circuit of an ε-cell.

Feed to all inputs z and v of the cells of the left boundary the
constants $z_{il} = 1$, $v_{il} = 0$. Then in the channel z the value $z' = 1$
will be retained till a $\vee \bar{t} = 1$ (which is equivalent to the condition
a $\geq$ t, see Table 3.1). In that cell where, for the first time,
a $\vee \bar{t} = 0$ (that is, a < t), z' takes the value 0, and retains it.

Table 3.1

a	t	a$\vee\bar{t}$ (a$\geq$t)	a$\bar{t}$ (a>t)
0	0	1	0
0	1	0	0
1	0	1	1
1	1	1	0

In the channel v the value $v' = 0$ is retained till $za\bar{t} = 0$. The
situation $za\bar{t} = 1$ can arise only when in all preceding positions the
inequality a $\geq$ t is satisfied (which ensures the condition z = 1),
and in the current position a > t (which ensures $a\bar{t} = 1$, see Table

3.1). In such a position, v' takes the value 1 and retains it. Clearly, this corresponds to the relation $A > T$. Note that the signal z may change in the further positions; indeed, if in some of the less significant digits the inequality $a < t$ is met, then in this digit the value $z' = 0$ will form, which will be retained.

Table 3.2 shows the combinations of signals at the right boundary of the DF-structure under consideration, corresponding to all six criteria of comparison.

Table 3.2

Result of comparison	Signals at the right boundary
$A_i = T$	$\bar{v}'z' = 1$
$A_i \neq T$	$v' \vee \bar{z}' = 1$
$A_i > T$	$v' = 1$
$A_i \geq T$	$v' \vee z' = 1$
$A_i < T$	$\bar{v}'\bar{z}' = 1$
$A_i \leq T$	$\bar{v}' = 1$

3.5.6. Between-The-Limits Searches (γ-structure)

In the memory elements of the cells a Boolean matrix A is stored from m n-bit numbers A_i $(i = 1,...,n)$. In addition, two n-bit numbers P and Q $(P < Q)$, the boundaries of the search interval, are given . All the elements A_i such that $P\ \theta_1\ A_i\ \theta_2\ Q$, where $\theta_1, \theta_2 \in \{ <, \leq, >, \geq \}$, have to be singled out.

The following algorithm is used. In each row the bit-wise comparison is made, beginning with the most significant digit, of the element $A_i = a_{i1}a_{i2}...a_{in}$ with the upper bound $Q = q_{i1}q_{i2}...q_{in}$, and simultaneously with the lower bound $P = p_{i1}p_{i2}...p_{in}$. If during the comparison of A_i with Q the first inequality encountered is $a > q$, then $A_i > Q$; that is, the result of the search is negative. If during the comparison of A_i with P the first inequality encountered is $a < p$, then $A_i < P$, which also corresponds to a negative result. In other cases, the result is positive; that is, the element A_i belongs to the given interval.

This algorithm can be implemented, for instance, by using the properties of the channels of the ε-structure discussed above. If a channel $z_1' = z_1(a \vee \bar{q})$ isorganized, then the signal $z_1 = 1$ will be ept in this channel till $a \geq q$. In the second channel $z_2' = z_2(\bar{a} \vee p)$, the signal $z_2 = 1$ will be kept till $a \leq p$. Then the result of the search can be produced by means of the third channel $v' = v \vee z_1 a \bar{q} \vee z_2 \bar{a} p$. Indeed, for the boundary signal $v_0 = 0$, the value of v' becomes 1 only in those cases when in the process of comparison the situation $a > q (z_1 a \bar{q} = 1)$ arises, or else $a < p$ ($z_2 \bar{a} p = 1$). These situations correspond to a negative result of the search. If, however, we have $v' = 0$ at the right boundary of the matrix, this means that the element contained in the corresponding row belongs to the given interval.

The system of logical functions of the cell is as follows:

$$z_1' = z_1 (a \vee \bar{q}),$$
$$z_2' = z_2 (\bar{a} \vee p),$$
$$v' = v \vee z_1 a \bar{q} \vee z_2 \bar{a} p,$$
$$p' = p,$$
$$q' = q.$$

3.5.7. Adjacency Searches (v-structure)

Different processors realizing nearest neighbours searches can be designed using the following reasoning.

Consider first the case of the nearest greater search. Comparing the elements of the array with the comparand X (simultaneously in all rows), mark in each row the position where the inequality $a > x$ is met for the first time. Then it suffices to find that of the marked rows, in which the mark takes the rightmost position (i.e. corresponds to the digit with minimal weight). The result will thus be found only in that row, since the difference $(A_i - X)$ is minimal in it.

In general, the right column may contain several marks, which means that the corresponding rows contain numbers for which the differences $(A_i - X)$ do not exceed 2^l (where l is the position of the right column). The result of the search should be the lowest of these numbers. Since in the most significant positions (up to the l-th inclusive) all numbers considered are equal, it suffices to find the minimum over $(l-1)$ lower bits. The result, the nearest greater number, is contained only in the row singled out in this way.

The first stage of the algorithm described can be realized, for instance, by means of the channels of the ε-structure.

The description of the ε-processor shows that the digit, where the inequality $a > x$ is met for the first time, is marked by the appearance of the signal $v' = 1$. In each of the rows singled out in this way the signal $v' = 1$ "departs" from the marked digit and runs to the right. The simplest way to choose the rows we are interested in (i.e. with differences not exceeding 2^l) from all these rows is to make each newly marked digit forbid propagation of the signals $v = 1$ in all rows where they appeared (at the left) before.

To realize the second stage of the algorithm, it is necessary to change the function of the second horizontal channel of the ε-structure to $v' = vt \lor z\overline{ax}$, to introduce an additional vertical channel $y' = y \lor z\overline{ax}$, and to connect in each column the inhibition bus t with the output of the vertical channel y'_m (through an inverter).

Indeed, if for $y_0 = 0$ a column contains at least one marked digit, i.e., such that $z\overline{ax} = 1$, then $y'_m = 1$, $t = 0$, and, consequently, the chain of a signal $v = 1$ will be cut in all those rows where it came from the left. At the same time, at the output of the cell of the marked digit in the current column (or maybe several marked digits simultaneously), due to the term $z\overline{ax}$, the signal $v' = 1$ appears again. This signal may be cut, in its turn, in one of the following positions. And it is only in the l-th column, when there can be no marked digits to the right in any row of the matrix, that the signal $v = 1$ will not be cut further by the signal $t = 0$.

The third, and last, stage of the algorithm consists in the search of the minimal (over the lower bits) from the numbers singled out at the second stage. This search can be implemented by means of channels realizing functions similar to those of the β-structure.

As the analysis of the rows begins in this case by the signal $v = 1$, the function of the channel v must be changed, accordingly, to $v' = v(\overline{a}\vee s)t \vee z\overline{a}x$. According to the algorithm of minimum search, the variable s should take the value 1 if all the digits analyzed in this column are ones. Thus, another vertical channel $r' = r \vee \overline{a}v$ and an auxiliary function $s_0 = \overline{r}'_m$ have to be introduced.

The complete system of logical functions of the new cell is as follows:

$$z' = z(a \vee \overline{x}), \qquad\qquad x' = x,$$
$$v' = v(\overline{a} \vee s)t \vee z\overline{a}x, \qquad s' = s,$$
$$y' = y \vee z\overline{a}x, \qquad\qquad t' = t,$$
$$r' = r \vee \overline{a}v, \qquad\qquad t_0 = \overline{y}'_m, \qquad s_o = \overline{r}'_{mi}$$

The values of the boundary signals are: $z_0 = 1$, $v_0 = 0$, $y_0 = 0$, $r_0 = 0$. The result of the search is determined by the value of the signal v' at the right boundary of the matrix: $v' = 1$ means that this row contains the number which is the nearest upper neighbour to the comparand.

The nearest smaller search is made similarly.

To this point, we have discussed in this Chapter DF-structures for direct implementation of various associative searches. We will consider now some more DF-structures with basic operations belonging to other classes of functions.

3.5.8. Component-Wise Comparison (η-structure)

Suppose two numerical vectors $\underline{A}$ and $\underline{B}$ are given. The problem is to compare them according to the relations $A_i\ \theta\ B_i$, where $\theta \in \{<, \leq, =, \neq, >, \geq\}$.

The result of the operation should be a binary vector with the i-th component "1", if the given relation is satisfied for the i-th components of argument vectors, and "0" otherwise.

For the hardware implementation of this problem an iterative circuit similar to that of the ε-structure can be used.

As was shown above, in each row of the ε-structure a one-dimensional iterative circuit is realized recognizing all possible relations between the elements stored in the rows of the matrix and a single comparand carried by the vertical buses x. The problem of component-wise comparison differs from the previous one in that each row has its own comparand, i.e. the corresponding component of the second vector. Thus, it can be solved by enlarging the matrix so that each cell contains two binary memory elements for storing the corresponding digits of the same components of vectors $\underline{A}$ and $\underline{B}$, and by introducing, instead of the variable x common for all rows, individual variables b:

$$z' = (a \lor \bar{b});$$
$$v' = v \lor za\bar{b}.$$

Boundary signals are: $z_0 = 1$, $v_0 = 0$.

The results are recognized by the values of the signals z' and v' at the right boundary of the matrix, similar to the ε-matrix.

3.5.9. Classification (ρ-structure)

The rows of the matrix of memory elements contain binary constants $X_1, X_2, ..., X_i, X_{i+1}$, ... written in increasing order, and the input register contains an arbitrary binary number A subject to classification. The processor must compare this number with all the constants and produce in the i-th row a definite signal if A belongs to the interval $[X_i, X_{i+1}]$.

The problem of classification is, in a sense, the inverse of the problem of search in the given interval. When an interval search is done, a set of numbers is analyzed for belonging to one interval, whereas when classification is done, the belonging of one number to one of a given set of intervals is established.

To solve the classification problem, an iterative circuit can be used similar to that of the γ-structure. In each row of the γ-processor the element A_i stored in the memory of this row is analyzed for belonging to an interval [P,Q], the boundaries of this interval being brought through vertical buses p and q.

When classification is done, the lower bound X_i is stored in the memory of the current row, the upper bound X_{i+1} in the memory of the nearest lower row, and the analyzed number A is brought bit-wise from the external register to the inputs of vertical buses a. To bring the binary codes of the upper bound, the output of the memory element of each cell must be connected to one of the inputs of the nearest upper cell. Denoting this input y , the system of logical functions of the cell of the present structure takes the form:

$$z'_1 = z_1 (a \lor x),$$
$$z'_2 = z_2 (\bar{a} \lor y),$$
$$v' = v \lor z_1 \bar{a}x \lor z_2 a\bar{y},$$
$$a' = a, \quad y' = x_{i+1}.$$

The boundary signals are: $z_{10} = z_{20} = 1$, $v_0 = 0$.

The presence of the signal v = 0 at the right boundary in the i-th row means that the given number A belongs to the interval $[X_i, X_{i+1}]$.

3.5.10. Compression (λ-structure)

Consider a two-dimensional iterative network (Fig.3.16) with two directions of propagation of signals, implementing the following transformations.

If an arbitrary binary vector is applied to the boundary inputs (say, of the left boundary), then in the first column the first "one" (from the top) of the given vector is singled out (i.e., marked by some special logical combination), in the second column the second "one" is singled out, and so on.

These transformations can be realized by means of two channels: the vertical $t' = z \lor t$ and horizontal $z' = zt$, if the given vector is fed to the boundary inputs z_{il} and the constants "0" are fed to all the boundary inputs t.

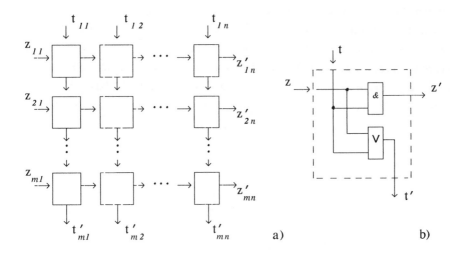

Fig.3.16. Compression of binary vectors: a) general structure
of λ-martrix; b) logic circuit of λ-cell.

Consider the first (left) column of a two-dimensional circuit with such channels (Fig.3.16). The variable t retains the value 0 in the vertical channel of this column only till $z = 0$. In some i_1-th cell, where $z = 1$ is encountered for the first time, the value of t changes to 1, which cannot change then till the lower bound. However, the i_1-th cell continues to receive the signal $t = 0$. Hence, it is the only cell in the whole column where the combination $z\bar{t} = 1$ is present. This combination will serve as an indication for extracting the "one".

The horizontal channel of the i_1-th cell thus indicated is closed by the signal $t = 0$; thus, the first "one" of the given vector does not propagate further along the current row. In all cells lower than the indicated one, $t = 1$, so that $z' = z$. Thus, a duplicate of the given vector is applied to the inputs of the second column, with the exception of its first "one".

Similar transformations are performed in the second, the third column, etc: in some i_2-th cell of the 2nd column the second "one" of the given vector is indicated, in some i_3-th cell of the 3rd column the third "one" is indicated, etc. ($i_1 < i_2 < ...$).

Clearly, signals "1" appear at the outputs t' of the lower bound in the 1st, 2nd,... columns of the λ-matrix, and the number of such columns corresponds to the number of ones in the given binary vector.

Hence, the λ-structure performs compression (see also Chapter 4).

CHAPTER 4

Functional Possibilities
of Distributed Functional Structures

Before we go on to describe the implementation of parallel homogeneous processors in computing systems, we will consider some functional properties of DF-structures. By demonstrating several statements concerning the multifunctionality of these structures, we will show that they realize certain useful data processing functions which do not follow immediately from their basic functions. This refers, first of all, to α- and λ- structures.

4.1. Analysis of α-structure

4.1.1. *Matrix Memory Unit*

Statement 1. *α-structure is a matrix memory unit with addressed writing and reading of data.*

Suppose an n-bit binary word $B = b_1 b_2 ... b_n$ has to be written into the i-th row of the α-matrix. Connect in the j-th column (j = 1,2,...,n) the boundary inputs x and y and apply to these inputs the corresponding bits of the word B: $x_{1j} = y_{1j} = b_j$.

Apply to all inputs z of the left boundary the constants $z_0 = 0$. Then, in accordance with (3.2), signals z = 0 will be set in all the cells of the α-matrix. Hence, in accordance with (3.3), the vertical channels x of each column will form a bus $x' = x$, which carries the values of the bits of the word B to the first inputs of the first write-in gates (see Fig.3.14.b) of all memory elements of the corresponding columns. At the same time, the negations of these variables are applied to the first inputs of second write-in gates.

Now, if the "write" signal $u = 1$ is applied to the boundary input u of the i-th row, then the word B will be written in the memory elements of this row.

The reset of data in any row (or in several rows) is made by means of writing into this row (or rows) a word $B = 00...0$.

To read the contents of the i-th row, it is sufficient to apply a word $B = 00...0$ to the memory inputs, and the "read" signal $z_{ii} = 1$ to the boundary input z of the i-th row. It is necessary also to ensure $z_{ki} = 0$ for all $k \neq i$. As in all the l-th rows of the matrix $(l < i)$ $z = 0$, the signals $x = y = 0$ are applied to the inputs x and y of all cells of the i-th row, as has been shown above. As the signal $z_{il} = 1$ is applied to the i-th row, $z = 1$ will be in all the cells of the i-th row, according to (3.2). Hence, according to (3.3), $x' = a$; that is, at the outputs x' of the cells of the i-th row appear the contents of corresponding memory elements of this row. As, by convention, $z = 0$ must be in all the further r-th rows $(r > i)$, the bus $x' = x$ is formed in each column of this lower part of the matrix, and the contents of the i-th row are transferred unchanged from the outputs x' of the i-th row to the outputs x' of the lower boundary of the matrix, which constitute the output ports of the memory unit. Thus, the α-structure enables arbitrary binary data to be written (read) into (from) its memory elements.

In contrast to the usual RAMs, in the α-structure some more complicated read and write operations can be performed. Consider the operations of duplication and disjunctive reading.

Simultaneous writing of a word B in the memory elements of two or more rows of the matrix will be called *duplication*.

From the description of the writing procedure above it follows that when signals $u = 1$ are simultaneously applied to the inputs of several rows, the α-structure implements duplication.

Another operation is defined as follows. Let a word B_k is written in the k-th row of the matrix, and a word B_l in the l-th row. We call *disjunctive reading* an operation producing at the outputs of the memory device the word B_{kvl}, each digit of which is the disjunction of corresponding digits of the words B_k and B_l. The operation of disjunctive reading generalizes naturally to the case of q rows $(2 \leq q \leq m)$.

From the description of the reading procedure above it follows that when signals $z = 1$ are simultaneously applied to the inputs z_{il} of several rows, the α-structure implements disjunctive reading. Indeed, the vertical channel x forms a disjunctive chain in each column of the α-matrix. Hence, when signals $z = 1$ are fed into several rows, then a disjunction of the contents of all memory elements of the current column of these rows is formed. This means that disjunctive reading is performed.

4.1.2. *Homogeneous Computing Media*

Statement 2. *α-structure is a reconfigurable homogeneous computing medium.*

When an α-structure is used as a specialized maximum search device, or as a matrix memory unit, the memory elements of the α-cells store binary digits of the given Boolean matrices (argument arrays). However, another, dual approach in using this structure is possible. In this approach the structure is considered as a homogeneous computing medium, the memory elements of its cells serving for reconfiguration.

From the expressions (3.2) to (3.5) it follows that functions realized by each α-cell depend on the values of variables a,x,y,z. As was shown above, the α-structure enables arbitrary binary information to be written into memory elements of cells. Thus, in the process of configuring, arbitrary values (0 or 1) can be prescribed to the independent variable a in each cell. As to the variables x,y,z, they can be fixed only at the inputs of the cells of the left and upper boundaries of the α-structure. The constants 0 and 1, fixed at the inputs y, are thus brought through the buses y directly to the inputs y of all the cells of corresponding columns. As to the values of z (corr. x) at the inputs of the cells not belonging to the left (corr. upper) boundary, they depend on the states of other cells. However, after the end of transition processes, at the inputs of each cell the values of variables x,y,z, uniquely defined by the boundary constants and the states of memory elements of some other cells, are established.

Consider the behaviour of the α-cell for the settings a = 0 and a = 1.

From (3.2) and (3.3) it follows that for a = 0:

$$x' = x, \quad z' = z\bar{y}. \qquad (4.1)$$

Hence, in this case in the channel z the *conjunction* of variables received at the inputs z and y is realized, with the simultaneous negation of the variable y. Such a cell will be called an α_{AND}-cell and denoted as shown in Fig.4.1.a.

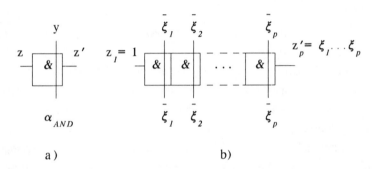

Fig.4.1. a) α_{AND}-cell; b) horizontal conjunction chain.

It is evident that the horizontal chain of p sequentially connected α_{AND}-cells (Fig.4.1.b) realizes on its output z'_p a p-input conjunction, if negations of independent variables ξ_j are applied to the inputs y_j (j = 1,...,p). At the same time, the variables ξ are fed by the buses y to the inputs y' of corresponding cells; this can be used for transferring data into cells of other rows in constructing two-dimensional structures.

In addition, in the α_{AND}-cell a vertical chain x' = x is formed, which may also be used for transferring signals downwards.

For a = 1:

$$x' = x \lor z, \quad z' = z. \qquad (4.2)$$

Hence, in the channel x the disjunction of variables received at the inputs x and z is realized. Such a cell will be called an α_{OR}-cell, and denoted as shown in Fig.4.2.a.

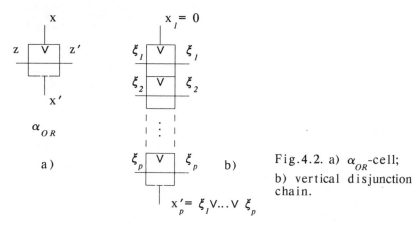

a)

b)

Fig.4.2. a) α_{OR}-cell;
b) vertical disjunction chain.

The vertical chain of p α_{OR}-cells (Fig.4.2.b) realizes on its output x'_p a p-input disjunction, if independent variables ξ_j are applied to the inputs z_i (i = 1,...,p), and the constant   0   is applied to the input x_1. In the same time, the variables ξ are fed along the chains   z'= z, appearing at this setting into the outputs z', and can be used in other columns in constructing two-dimensional structures. The functioning of the α_{OR}-cell   does not depend   on   y; hence, the bus y can be used separately.

Now let, for   a = 0, the value of variable   y = 0   be fixed in an α-cell. Then (4.1) takes the form   x'= x,   z'= z, that is,   the cell realizes the functions of a four-terminal interconnection element ("transfer"), with the following adjacency matrix:

$$
\begin{array}{c c}
 & \begin{array}{cccc} x & x' & z & z' \end{array} \\
\begin{array}{c} x \\ x' \\ z \\ z' \end{array} &
\left[\begin{array}{cccc}
0 & 1 & 0 & 0 \\
0 & 0 & 0 & 0 \\
0 & 0 & 0 & 1 \\
0 & 0 & 0 & 0
\end{array} \right] .
\end{array}
$$

56

Such a cell will be called an α_{TR}-cell, and denoted as shown in Fig.4.3.a.

The α_{TR}-cell is used for independent signal transferring in two perpendicular directions: downwards $(x'= x)$ and from left to right $(z'= z)$. Note that when a cell is in this mode, the bus y contains 0, which can affect the behaviour of other cells of the corresponding column.

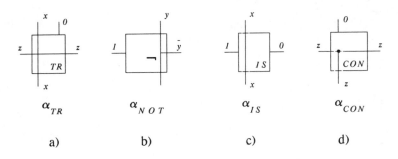

$$\alpha_{TR} \qquad \alpha_{NOT} \qquad \alpha_{IS} \qquad \alpha_{CON}$$

a)   b)   c)   d)

Fig.4.3. Different interconnection α-cells.

If for $a = 0$ the value of the variable $z = 1$ is fixed, then (4.1) takes the form: $x'= x$, $z'= \bar{y}$. Such a cell realizes also the functions of an interconnection element, which turns to the right the signal coming along the bus y. At the same time, this element may be considered as a functional element implementing inversion. Also,signals can be transferred downwards through the chain $x'= x$. The adjacency matrix of this element may be represented as follows:

$$
\begin{array}{c}
 \\
x \\
x' \\
y \\
y' \\
z \\
z'
\end{array}
\begin{array}{cccccc}
x & x' & y & y' & z & z' \\
\left[\begin{array}{cccccc}
0 & 1 & 0 & 0 & 0 & 0 \\
0 & 0 & 0 & 0 & 0 & 0 \\
0 & 0 & 0 & 1 & 0 & \bar{1} \\
0 & 0 & 1 & 0 & 0 & \bar{1} \\
0 & 0 & 0 & 0 & 0 & 0 \\
0 & 0 & 0 & 0 & 0 & 0
\end{array}\right] .
\end{array}
$$

The negation sign denotes here the inversion of the signal in the corresponding channel. This element may be considered also as a functional element implementing the inversion.

Such a cell will be called an α_{NOT}-cell, and denoted in logical circuits as shown in Fig.4.3.b.

Note that when a cell is in this mode, $z = 1$ is fixed, which can affect the behaviour of other cells in the same row to the left.

If for $a = 0$ the value of the variable $y = 1$ is fixed, then (4.1) takes the form $x' = x$, $z' = 0$. We get then an interconnection element with the adjacency matrix:

$$
\begin{array}{c}
\quad\;\; \begin{array}{cccc} x & x' & z & z' \end{array} \\
\begin{array}{c} x \\ x' \\ z \\ z' \end{array}
\left[
\begin{array}{cccc}
0 & 1 & 0 & 0 \\
0 & 0 & 0 & 0 \\
0 & 0 & 0 & 0 \\
0 & 0 & 0 & 0
\end{array}
\right] .
\end{array}
$$

This element transfers the signals vertically $(x' = x)$, and "isolates" all cells to the right in the same row $(z = 0)$. We shall call such an element an α_{IS}-cell, and denote it in the circuits as shown in Fig.4.3.c.

At this setting, the bus y transfers the signal $y = 1$ which can affect the behaviour of other cells of the column.

Another interconnection element can be obtained at the mode $a = 1$, $x = 0$. From (4.2) it follows that $x' = z$, $z' = z$.

The adjacency matrix is:

$$
\begin{array}{c}
\quad\;\; \begin{array}{cccccc} x & x' & y & y' & z & z' \end{array} \\
\begin{array}{c} x \\ x' \\ y \\ y' \\ z \\ z' \end{array}
\left[
\begin{array}{cccccc}
0 & 0 & 0 & 0 & 0 & 0 \\
0 & 0 & 0 & 0 & 0 & 0 \\
0 & 0 & 0 & 1 & 0 & 0 \\
0 & 0 & 1 & 0 & 0 & 0 \\
0 & 1 & 0 & 0 & 0 & 1 \\
0 & 0 & 0 & 0 & 0 & 0
\end{array}
\right] .
\end{array}
$$

This cell is an interconnection element of the type "connection", realizing the branching of the signal coming into the horizontal chain $z' = z$, directing it simultaneously along the vertical $(x' = z)$.

We shall call such an element an α_{CON}-cell, and denote it in the circuits as shown in Fig.4.3.d.

To put an element into the last mode, it is necessary to fix $x = 0$. This can affect the behaviour of other cells above in the same column.

Since the functions of an α_{CON}-cell do not depend on y, the bus y can be used for other purposes.

Thus, for different states of the memory element, and different values of the variables x, y, z, the cells of the α-structure can behave as functional or interconnection elements. Hence, the α-structure is a reconfigurable homogeneous computing medium.

It should be noted that, in contrast to the universal computing media [83], in an α-structure, essentially a specialized one, there are some restrictions to embedding arbitrary logical circuits in it. Thus, transferring of signals to the right and downwards is allowed, whereas there are no means to transfer them to the left; there is a connection between the chains z and x, but none between x and y or x and z.

4.1.3. *Logical Functions*

Statement 3. *In an α-structure of size $(2n - 1) * 2^{n-1}$ an arbitrary logical function of n variables can be implemented.*

It is known that an arbitrary logical function of n variables can be represented in a principal disjunctive normal form (PDNF) as follows:

$$f(\xi_1, \xi_2, \ldots, \xi_n) = \bigvee_{f(\sigma_1, \sigma_2, \ldots, \sigma_n) = 1} \xi_1^{\sigma_1} \xi_2^{\sigma_2} \ldots \xi_n^{\sigma_n},$$

where $\xi_i^{\sigma_i} = \begin{cases} \xi_i, & \text{if } \sigma_i = 1, \\ \bar{\xi}_i, & \text{if } \sigma_i = 0, \end{cases}$

and the disjunction on the right is taken upon all sets $<\sigma_1, \sigma_2, ..., \sigma_n>$ at which the function f equals one. The number of minterms on the right equals $k \leq 2^n$.

As shown above, any elementary conjunction can be realized by means of a row of α_{AND}-cells of corresponding length. In the general case, each variable can enter the PDNF either in a straight, or an inverted, form. Hence, to realize simultaneously all elementary conjunctions, we need an α-matrix with row length $2n$. This matrix should have 2^n rows, because the maximal number of elementary conjunctions is 2^n.

The variables ξ_i and their negations are fed to the inputs y of the upper boundary. Due to the commutativity of conjunction, the distribution of the variables between the columns is arbitrary. We assume, for definiteness, that the variables ξ_i and $\bar{\xi}_i$ are arranged as shown in Fig.4.4.

To realize a certain conjunction in some row of the α-matrix, it is sufficient to set all its cells in accordance with the values of σ_i. That is, if $\sigma_i = 0$, then the cell which is set onto the function α_{AND} $(a = 0)$ is that corresponding to ξ_i; if $\sigma_i = 1$, then, on contrary, the cell which is set onto α_{AND} is that corresponding to $\bar{\xi}_i$. All other cells of the same row are set onto the function α_{OR} $(a = 1)$ and serve only for horizontal connection (via the chain $z' = z$) of all those cells α_{AND} which are really used to calculate the value of the minterm.

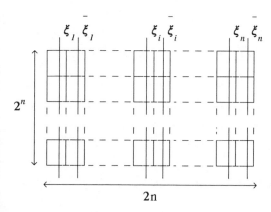

Fig.4.4. Implementation of minterms in α-matrix.

It follows from this construction that (for boundary constant $z_I = 1$) the signals $z_n' = 1$ at the right boundary of the row is formed if and only if for all variables entering the given elementary conjunction holds $\xi_i = \sigma_i$, that is, if it is equal to 1.

Now, supplement the considered α-matrix at the right by one column of α_{OR}-cells. As was shown, such a column implements a disjunction of variables fed to the inputs z of all its cells. Hence (for boundary constant x = 0) at the output of this column the disjunction of all minterms, that is, the given function $f(\xi_1, \xi_2, ..., \xi_n)$, is realized.

Clearly, one can reduce the complexity of an α-structure realizing logical functions if, instead of principal DNFs, one uses minimal DNFs. The most complicated logical function of n variables has, in its minimal DNF, 2^{n-1} minterms of n variables, including each variable in both the direct and the negated form. Hence, the upper bound for the complexity of realization of logical functions in an α-structure is $(2n + 1)*2^{n-1}$.

Thus, Statement 3 is proved.

Statement 4. *In an α-structure of size $(2n + 1)*2^{n-1}$ an arbitrary system of 1 logical functions of n variables can be implemented.*

The proof is similar to that given above.

4.1.4. *Associative Memory*

Statement 5. *In an α-structure of size 2mn an associative memory of capacity of m n-bit words can be implemented.*

Before we prove this, note that the α-structure is somewhat similar to the classical CAM; however, it does not perform immediately the basic operation of a CAM, the equality search. To demonstrate the possibility of using the α-structure as a CAM, we introduce the notion of pα-element.

A part of an α-structure formed by p adjacent α-cells of a row is called pα-element.

We go on now to the proof of Statement 5.

Consider the functions implemented by a 2α-element (Fig.4.5.). From (3.2) it follows that:

$$z'_2 = z_1(a_1 \vee \bar{y}_1)\,(a_2 \vee \bar{y}_2) = z_1(a_1 a_2 \vee a_1\bar{y}_2 \vee a_2\bar{y}_1 \vee \bar{y}_1\bar{y}_2). \quad (4.3)$$

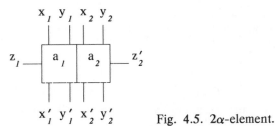

Fig. 4.5. 2α-element.

Assume that, in using an α-structure as an associative memory, data are stored in memory elements in the two-phase code (one bit in each 2α-element), according to the rule shown in Table 4.1.

Table 4.1. ENCODING OF BITS.

Bit value	Contents of 2α-element	
	a_1	a_2
0	0	1
1	1	0

Clearly for such encoding $a_1 \neq a_2$, and the expression (4.3) takes the form:

$$z'_2 = z_1(a_1\bar{y}_2 \vee a_2\bar{y}_1 \vee \bar{y}_1\bar{y}_2) = z_1 g,$$

where

$$g = a_1\bar{y}_2 \vee a_2\bar{y}_1 \vee \bar{y}_1\bar{y}_2.$$

Build the truth table of the function g (Table 4.2.)

Table 4.2. TRUTH TABLE OF FUNCTION g.

a_1	0	0	0	0	1	1	1	1
y_1	0	0	1	1	0	0	1	1
y_2	0	1	0	1	0	1	0	1
g	1	1	0	0	1	0	1	0

As follows from this table, for $y_1 = y_2 = 0$, we have $z'_2 = z_1$, independently of the values of a_1 and a_2. Thus, the combination $y_1 = 0$, $y_2 = 0$ in all cases ensures passing of the signal through the 2α-element. Since in an α-structure the bus y traverses all the cells of each column, this holds for the corresponding 2α-elements of all rows of the matrix. Hence, the combination "00" at the inputs y may be used for masking the corresponding bit of the two-phase memory unit.

Then, in accordance with the above table, for $y_1 = y_2$ we have $z'_2 = z_1$ if and only if:

for $a_1 = 0$ (code 01), $y_1 = 0$, $y_2 = 1$;
for $a_1 = 1$ (code 10), $y_1 = 1$, $y_2 = 0$.

It follows that, if the bits of the comparand are encoded in the same way as the data stored in the α-matrix, and if the comparand is fed to the inputs y of the upper bound of the α-matrix, then (for boundary constants $z_{i\,1} = 1$ at all the inputs z of the left boundary) the signal $z' = 1$ will appear at the outputs z' of the right boundary in those, and only those, rows where the values of unmasked bits coincide with those of corresponding bits of the comparand.

Thus, for the encoding used above, the α-structure realizes the functions of an associative memory. Since two α-cells are used here to store each bit, each n-bit word requires an α-row of length 2n for its storage.

This proves Statement 5.

4.1.5. *Programmable Logic Array*

Statement 6. *In an α-structure of size $(2s + t)*q$ a programmable logic array with s inputs, t outputs, and q standard product terms can be implemented.*

A programmable logic array (PLA) is known to consist of two logical structures. The first of these, called the "AND-matrix", forms q standard product terms F_1, F_2,..., F_q of s input variables (with or without negations), and the second, called the "OR-matrix", realizes t disjunctions of the terms produced by the AND-matrix.

As was shown above, when two-phase encoding is used, an α-structure of size $2s*q$ realizes on the outputs z' of corresponding rows q minterms of s variables, if the input sets x_1, x_2,..., x_s are fed to the inputs of corresponding columns. Here two states, 01 and 10 , are used for encoding the variables stored in the memory elements of the α-structure.

The special feature of the AND matrix of a PLA is that it uses representation of product terms in a ternary form. The third, "don't care" state means that the term considered takes the value 1, independently of the value (0 or 1) of the variable, encoded by the "don't care" code in the input set.

We now show that the two-phase encoding in an α-structure ensures representation of "don't-care" states. In Table 4.3 the possible states of an 2α-element and their notations are shown.

The states 0 and 1 are used as above, for encoding a variable entering the given term in complemented (0) or direct (1) form. From (4.3) it follows that for $a_1 = a_2 = 1$ $z'_2 = z_1$, independently of the values of outer variables y_1 and y_2. Hence, the code X ("11") corresponds to the state "don't care" of the given term relative to the given variable, which is only required to realize the functions of the AND-matrix of the PLA.

As to the OR-matrix, according to what was shown above, an α-structure of size $q*t$ implements t arbitrary disjunctions of q variables fed to the inputs z of its left boundary, which entirely

64

Table 4.3. FOUR STATES OF 2α-ELEMENT

Contents of 2α-element		State
a_1	a_2	
0	1	0
1	0	1
1	1	X
0	0	Y

corresponds to the functions of an OR-matrix of the PLA. In the present case the outputs z' of the right boundary of the field of the α-structure used as an AND-matrix can be identified with the inputs z of the left boundary of the field used as an OR-matrix.

Thus, an α-structure of size $(2s*q) + (q*t) = (2s + t)*q$ implements a PLA with parameters s,q,t, which is what what was to be proved.

Note that the α-structure allows flexible writing and reading of data (see the Statement 1). Hence, a PLA implemented in an α-structure is *reprogrammable*.

4.1.6. *Functional Memory*

Statement 7. *In an α-structure of size* $2mn$ *a functional memory of* m n-*bit words can be implemented.*

The notion of functional memory (FM), being a generalization of PLA, was introduced by Gardner [30]. Whereas the PLA realizes only Boolean functions represented in DNFs, the FM, in combination with some simple input and output transformers, ensures representation of bracket forms.

The essential difference between FM and PLA is that each memory element of FM can take four internal states. As can be seen from Table 4.3., two-phase encoding in an α-structure ensures setting of each of the 2α-elements in any of the four states. This proves Statement 7.

To illustrate the possibilities of FM, consider a scheme using as output transformers XOR gates.

In constructing a PLA, a DNF in the OR-matrix is implemented by *one column of α-cells*, with the following simple encoding: "1" in the cells corresponding to minterms entering the given DNF, and "0" in the other cells.

Unlike the construction of an FM with output transformers, *columns of 2α-elements* should be used in the OR-matrix. Consider a column of 2α-elements, the outputs x' of which are connected to the inputs of a XOR element (Fig.4.6.). Constants "0" are fed to the inputs x and y of the upper boundary, of which $x = 0$ ensures proper operation of the disjunctive chain, and $y = 0$ the independent propagation of the output signal of the AND-matrix along the paths of the OR-matrix (because for $y = 0$ we have $z' = z$ independently of the setting).

Each 2α-element of the column can be set into any of the four states (see Table 4.3). If some conjunction F does not enter at all into the output function Φ, then the corresponding 2α-element should be set to the state "00"; that is, the code Y corresponds in the OR-matrix to the "don't care" state. If for some conjunctions F_{i1}, F_{i2}, ... all the corresponding 2α-elements of the column of the OR-matrix are set to the state "10" (or all to the state "01"), then we get:

$$\Phi = (F_{i1} \lor F_{i2} \lor ...) \oplus 0 = F_{i1} \lor F_{i2} \lor ...,$$

that is, the same function as in the case of simple disjunctive columns.

66

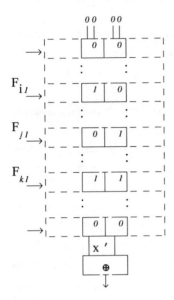

Fig.4.6. Settings of 2α-elements
in the OR-matrix of the
functional memory.

If, however, some 2α-elements are set to the state "10", and some
others to the state "01", then the basis is essentially enlarged. In
this case, at the output of the XOR element the function

$$\Phi' = (F_{i1} \lor F_{i2} \lor ...) \oplus (F_{j1} \lor F_{j2} \lor ...)$$

is realized.

Moreover, use of the code X ("11") allows us to introduce into the
basis the "inhibition" function. Indeed, if a 2α-element of the OR-
matrix is set to the state "11", and the input z of the
corresponding row is initiated by a signal coming from the AND-
matrix, then the function implemented at the output of the XOR element
of this column becomes zero independently of the states of other
2α-elements, as well as of the inputs of the OR-matrix. Therefore, for
instance, for the setting shown in Fig.4.6., the function Φ has the
form:

$$\Phi'' = [(F_{i1} \lor F_{i2} \lor ...) \oplus (F_{j1} \lor F_{j2} \lor ...)] \& \bar{F}_{k1} \& \bar{F}_{k2} \& ...$$

4.2. Analysis of λ-structure

4.2.1. *Unitary Coding*

To demonstrate some of the functional properties of λ-structures connected with their basic operation, *compression of the binary vector* (or "weighting"), we need some definitions from unitary coding theory.

A *unitary code* is a code in which a number is represented by a sequence of zeros and ones (a code word), so that the number of ones equals the represented number.

The number of ones in a code word of length n will be denoted Q_n^I and the number of zeros Q_n^0. Clearly, $Q_n^0 = n - Q_n^I$.

One well known example of unitary coding is the pulse representation of data, widely used in automatic control and measurement techniques. Unitary coding is a non-positional number notation.

In the general case, the ones of a unitary code may be arbitrarily interleaved with zeros. Such a code is called *sparse*. All sparse unitary codes with the same value of Q_n^I are equivalent, in the sense that they represent the same number.

A unitary code in which all the ones form a compact block without interspersed zeros is called *compressed*.

A compressed unitary code in which the block of ones takes the side position, on the left (or on the right), is called *normalized*. This corresponds to what Iverson called prefix (or suffix) vectors [51].

Example.

The number 7 in a sparse unitary code (for n = 16) may be represented as follows:

0010110111000010.

Clearly there are many such representations.

The number 7 in a compressed unitary code has the form:

0001111111000000,

with many other possible representations.

The number 7 in a Normalized Unitary Code (NUC) has two representations:

1111111000000000   and   0000000001111111.

We shall use also the Unit Positional Code (UPC), that is the code in which a number p is represented by a single "one" taking the $(p + 1)$-th position in the code word, the first (left) position being reserved for $p = 0$.

For example, the number 7 in UPC (for $n = 16$) has the form:

0000000100000000.

This coding is used in practice in the phase-pulse representation of data.

4.2.2. *Digital Compressors*

In logical data processing, the binary vectors and the codes they represent are transformed differently. Such transformations will be denoted $TR(A \rightarrow B)$, where A and B are conventional signs for the source and target codes (binary vectors) correspondingly.

An example of a transformation of importance in applications is the transformation of a sparse unitary code into a normalized one. The operation performing this transformation will be called *compression*. A functional unit with compression as the basic operation will be called a *digital compressor*.

Statement 8. *λ-structure is a digital compressor.*

The correctness of this Statement follows immediately from the algorithm of synthesis of a λ-structure (see Chapter 3).

Now we consider some other schemes of digital compressors.

In Fig.4.7. is shown a pipelined scheme of a digital compressor which it is reasonable to use in cases when consecutive compressions of many binary vectors are required. The signals are propagated in three directions, from left to right, upwards and downwards. Each cell contains one flip-flop, and a combinational circuit realizing the functions $s = xz \vee yz$, where s is the set signal of the flip-flop. For a cell with coordinates (i,j):

$$x_{ij} = z'_{i+1, j-1} \; ; \; y_{ij} = z'_{i-1, j-1} \; ; \; z_{ij} = z'_{i, j-1} \; .$$

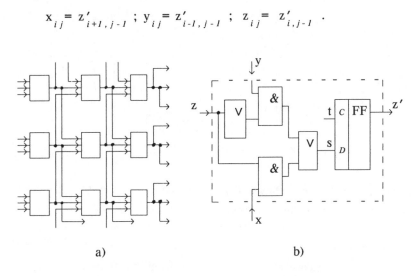

a)   b)

Fig.4.7. Pipelined digital compressor: a) general structure; b) logic circuit of a cell.

A clock pulse is applied in each cycle to the inputs t of each flip-flop of the compressor. To the inputs x of all cells of the bottom boundary are fed the constants "1"; to the inputs y of all cells of the upper boundary are fed the constants "0".

The operation of the pipelined compressor is based on the following idea. Each cell analyzes the content of three flip-flops located in the adjacent left column, in three neighbouring rows: that of the cell, the next upper, and the next lower. If in the preceding column just below a "one" was a "zero", then in the current column the corresponding "one" is pushed down one position and replaces the "zero" that was below it. Thus, in each cycle a binary vector is rewritten into the next column of the compressor, so that all "ones" which it was possible to push down are lowered one position. Obviously, any binary vector of dimension n may be thus compressed in (n - 1) cycles, at most, and the result will be in the (n - 1)-th column.

To explain the operation of this algorithm, consider the truth table of the function s (Table 4.4.).

Table 4.4. TRUTH TABLE OF FUNCTION s.

	1	2	3	4	5	6	7	8
y	0	0	0	0	1	1	1	1
z	0	0	1	1	0	0	1	1
x	0	1	0	1	0	1	0	1
s	0	0	0	1	1	1	0	1

From this table it follows that when a binary vector is transferred into the next column, then in each row:

- a "one" becomes a "zero", if just below it was a "zero" (sets 3 and 7);
- a "zero" becomes a "one", if just above it was a "one" (sets 5 and 6).
- data are transferred unchanged in other cases (sets 1,2,4,8).

In Fig.4.8 an example of compression for the binary vector $V = 0100110010$ ($n = 10$) is shown. In this case, the compression ends on the 5th cycle, because in the initial vector there were only 5 "zeros" below the upper "one". In the worst case (for $n = 10$) for the vector 1000000000, nine cycles would be needed.

Consecutive compression of a set of binary vectors in a pipelined compressor is performed as follows.

As in the 2nd cycle the partially transformed 1st vector is transferred to the 2nd column, the 2nd of the given set of vectors can be fed to the inputs of the 1st column. In the 3rd cycle, the 1st vector is transferred into the 3rd column, the 2nd vector into the 2nd column, and the 3rd vector of the given set can be fed to the inputs of the 1st column.

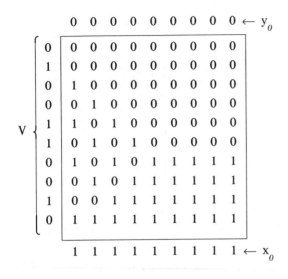

$$0 \quad 0 \quad 0 \quad 0 \quad 0 \quad 0 \quad 0 \quad 0 \quad 0 \leftarrow y_0$$

0	0	0	0	0	0	0	0	0	0
1	0	0	0	0	0	0	0	0	0
0	1	0	0	0	0	0	0	0	0
0	0	1	0	0	0	0	0	0	0
1	1	0	1	0	0	0	0	0	0
1	0	1	0	1	0	0	0	0	0
0	1	0	1	0	1	1	1	1	1
0	0	1	0	1	1	1	1	1	1
1	0	0	1	1	1	1	1	1	1
0	1	1	1	1	1	1	1	1	1

V

$$1 \quad 1 \quad 1 \quad 1 \quad 1 \quad 1 \quad 1 \quad 1 \quad 1 \leftarrow x_0$$

Fig.4.8. Example of pipelined compression.

Beginning with the $(n - 1)$-th cycle, at the outputs of the $(n - 1)$-th column will be consecutively produced (with a period τ, where τ is the cycle duration) the results of compression of the 1st, 2nd, etc. initial vectors.

The scheme of the compressor considered above (Fig.4.7.) was designed on the basis of direct simulation of the process of "pushing down" the "ones" of the given binary word. Another way to design the scheme of a compressor is the conventional approach of automata theory; that is, the scheme is considered as a system of n Boolean functions of n variables realizing the necessary transformations.

Consider a recurrent design procedure of a compressor.

Begin with the simplest compressor $(n = 2)$, shown in Fig.4.9.a. In the truth table below (Table 4.5), the inputs of this compressor are denoted by variables x_1, y_1, and the functions z_1, z_2 correspond to the 1st and the 2nd bits of the normalized unitary code at the outputs.

According to this table, $z_1 = x_1 \vee y_1$, $z_2 = x_1 y_1$.

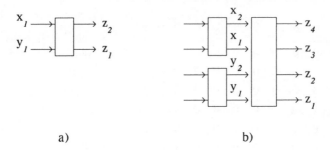

a)   b)

Fig.4.9. Simple compressors: a) for $n = 2$; b) for $n = 4$.

Now, consider the case $n = 4$ (Fig. 4.9.b). If x_1, x_2 and y_1, y_2 are the outputs of the two-input compressors of the preceding stage, then the truth table of the four-input compressor can be written as in Table 4.6. From this table, after minimization, the following system of logic functions is derived:

$$z_1 = x_1 \vee y_1,$$
$$z_2 = x_1 y_1 \vee x_2 \vee y_2,$$
$$z_3 = x_1 y_2 \vee x_2 y_1,$$
$$z_4 = x_2 y_2.$$

Table 4.5

x_1	y_1	z_2	z_1
0	0	0	0
0	1	0	1
1	0	0	1
1	1	1	1

Table 4.6

x_2	x_1	y_2	y_1	z_4	z_3	z_2	z_1
0	0	0	0	0	0	0	0
0	0	0	1	0	0	0	1
0	1	0	0	0	0	0	1
0	1	0	1	0	0	1	1
0	0	1	1	0	0	1	1
1	1	0	0	0	0	1	1
0	1	1	1	0	1	1	1
1	1	0	1	0	1	1	1
1	1	1	1	1	1	1	1

It can be shown that for the compressor the following rule holds.

Let the indexes of input variables x (y) correspond to the numbers of outputs of the first (second) compressor of the preceding stage, and the indexes of output functions z to the numbers of outputs of the considered stage. Then for each (j-th) stage of the compressor the expression of each function z_i (i = 1,...,2^j) is a disjunction of all prime implicants for which the sum of indexes of variables of each implicant equals i.

Using this rule, the system of functions z_i for any stage of the compressor is readily written. For instance, for j = 3 we have:

$$z_1 = x_1 \vee y_1 ,$$
$$z_2 = x_1 y_1 \vee x_2 \vee y_2 ,$$
$$z_3 = x_1 y_2 \vee x_2 y_1 \vee x_3 \vee y_3 ,$$
$$z_4 = x_1 y_3 \vee x_2 y_2 \vee x_3 y_1 \vee x_4 \vee y_4 ,$$
$$z_5 = x_1 y_4 \vee x_2 y_3 \vee x_3 y_2 \vee x_4 y_1 ,$$
$$z_6 = x_2 y_4 \vee x_3 y_3 \vee x_4 y_2 ,$$
$$z_7 = x_3 y_4 \vee x_4 y_3 ,$$
$$z_8 = x_4 y_4 .$$

In Fig 4.10. is shown the structure of such a compressor, called *logarithmic*. It is clear from the construction that the n-input logarithmic compressor contains $\log_2 n$ stages, which explains its name.

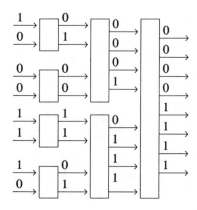

Fig.4.10. Logarithmic compressor for n = 8.

4.2.3. *Code Transformers*

In designing various data processing devices based on DF-structures, it is necessary to transform codes of different data representation systems (binary, unitary, unit positional, etc.). Consider some ways of constructing such transformers.

Transformer TR(2→UC) is shown in Fig.4.11. This simplest transformation is performed by means of forking wires, in accordance with the weights of binary digits of the input number. Such a scheme may be called a "wired tree".

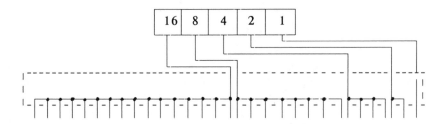

Fig. 4.11. Transformer (2→UC).

Transformer TR(2→UPC) is the usual, widely applied, binary decoder.

Transformer TR(UPC→2), the inverse of the preceding, is the binary coder, for which also many different realizations are known.

In the next Chapter we shall consider some coders and decoders implemented in α-structure.

Transformer TR(2→NUC). To perform this transformation, the sequence of two transformations discussed above can be used:

$$TR(2 \to NUC) \equiv TR(2 \to UC), \ TR(UC \to NUC).$$

Of interest also is a circuit performing an immediate transformation $TR(2 \to NUC)$. As in the case of the logarithmic compressor, consider the truth tables and the corresponding (minimized) systems of DNFs for the transformers $TR(2 \to NUC)$, with 1, 2, and 3 inputs (correspondingly, 1, 3, 7 outputs). In the present case, the tables simply reflect the coding rules, indexes of the variables corresponding to the weights of digits of the binary input code, and indexes of the functions to the numbers of positions of the output NUC. The system of DNF for the j-th stage evidently contains 2^j-1 functions of j variables.

Thus, for j = 1,2,3:

x_1	z_1
0	0
1	1

$z_1 = x_1.$

x_2	x_1	z_3	z_2	z_1
0	0	0	0	0
0	1	0	0	1
1	0	0	1	1
1	1	1	1	1

$z_1 = x_1 \lor x_2,$
$z_2 = x_2,$
$z_3 = x_1 \; x_2.$

x_4	x_2	x_1	z_7	z_6	z_5	z_4	z_3	z_2	z_1
0	0	0	0	0	0	0	0	0	0
0	0	1	0	0	0	0	0	0	1
0	1	0	0	0	0	0	0	1	1
0	1	1	0	0	0	0	1	1	1
1	0	0	0	0	0	1	1	1	1
1	0	1	0	0	1	1	1	1	1
1	1	0	0	1	1	1	1	1	1
1	1	1	1	1	1	1	1	1	1

$z_1 = x_1 \lor x_2 \lor x_4,$
$z_2 = x_2 \lor x_4,$
$z_3 = x_1 x_2 \lor x_4,$
$z_4 = x_4,$
$z_5 = (x_1 \lor x_2) \; x_4,$
$z_6 = x_2 \; x_4,$
$z_7 = x_1 x_2 \; x_4.$

Observing these systems of DNF, one can deduce the following rules.

If a system of DNFs for the (j-1)-th stage of the transformer TR(2→NUC) is given, then the construction of the systems of DNFs for the j-th stage is as follows:

a). For i = 1,2,...,$(2^{j-1}-1)$, the i-th function of the system is formed from the i-th function of the system of functions of the (j-1)-th stage by logical summation of it with the j-th variable;

b). For i = $(2^{j-1}+1)$,...,(2^j-1), the i-th function of the system is formed from the i-th function of the system of functions of the   (j-1)--th stage by logical multiplication of it with the   j-th variable;

c). For $i = 2^{j-1}$,   the   i-th function of the system coincides with the j-th   variable.

In the systems considered above, the corresponding subsystems are outlined by a dotted curve.

Using this rule, the system of functions for any   j   can be readily constructed.

For instance, for j = 4, we have:

$$z_1 = x_1 \vee x_2 \vee x_4 \vee x_8,$$
$$z_2 = x_2 \vee x_4 \vee x_8,$$
$$z_3 = x_1 x_2 \vee x_4 \vee x_8,$$
$$z_4 = x_4 \vee x_8,$$
$$z_5 = (x_1 \vee x_2) x_4 \vee x_8,$$
$$z_6 = x_2 x_4 \vee x_8,$$
$$z_7 = x_1 x_2 x_4 \vee x_8,$$
$$z_8 = x_8,$$
$$z_9 = (x_1 \vee x_2 \vee x_4) \, x_8,$$
$$z_{10} = (x_2 \vee x_4) \, x_8,$$
$$z_{11} = (x_1 x_2 \vee x_4) \, x_8,$$
$$z_{12} = x_4 \, x_8,$$
$$z_{13} = (x_1 \vee x_2) x_4 \, x_8,$$
$$z_{14} = x_2 x_4 \, x_8,$$
$$z_{15} = x_1 x_2 x_4 \, x_8.$$

The transformer $TR(2{\rightarrow}NUC)$ for   j = 4, constructed in accordance with these   systems   of   logic   functions,   is   shown   in   Fig.4.12.   The transformers $TR(2{\rightarrow}NUC)$ are constructed similarly for any   j.

Transformer (NUC→UPC) can be realized as a one-dimensional iterative circuit   (Fig.4.13.),   each   cell   of   which   implements   the   functions $z = x\bar{y}$ and $y' = x$. The transformer of   n-bit NUC must have   n+1 cells. The initial unitary code is fed to the inputs   x of the 1st, 2nd, ..., n-th cell. To the input   y   of the first cell the constant "0" is fed,   and to the input   x of the   (n+1)-th   cell, the constant

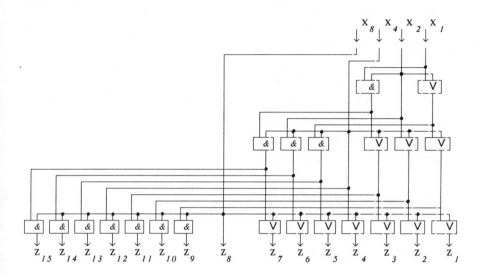

Fig.4.12. Transformer (2→NUC).

"1". The transformer "scans" the NUC from right to left. Until the zeros of the NUC come to the inputs x, the cells produce z = 0. In the single cell which corresponds to the first non-zero digit of the transformed code, the combination x = 1, y = 0 appears, and the signal z = x$\bar{y}$ = 1 is produced. In all other cells again z = 0. Thus, at the outputs z the UPC equivalent to the initial NUC is realized.

If the NUC contains no ones, then z = 1 is produced at the output of the (n+1)-th cell (due to the constant x = 1), which corresponds to the representation of zero in UPC.

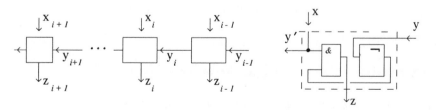

Fig.4.13. Transformer (NUC→UPC).

Transformer (UPC→NUC) is the inverse of the preceding. It is also a one-dimensional iterative circuit (Fig.4.14.). but in this case each cell realizes a different function: $v' = v\bar{x} \vee \bar{v}x$. Here x is the input signal, and v is the inter-element signal. The output signal is $z = v'$. The outputs $z_1,...,z_n$ correspond to the 1st,...,n-th digits of the NUC produced. The input x_0 is not used, as for $x_0 = 1$ (UPC of zero) all z must be zeros. If the constant $v_0 = 1$ is fed to the input v of the 1st cell, then the signal $v' = 1$ will be kept, till zeros are fed to the inputs x.

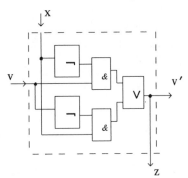

Fig.4.14. Transformer (UPC→NUC).

If in some cell there is $x = 1$ (which is possible for a single cell), then in this cell the signal $v' = 0$ is produced, which is kept in the sequel. As $z = v'$, the transformation (UPC→NUC) is realized.

Thus, we have considered some transformations between unitary codes and unit positional codes or usual binary codes. The characteristic feature of all these transformations is the conservation of the numerical equivalent of presented numbers. For each of the transformations different structural schemes may be used. Some transformations can be expressed as sequences, or chains, of others; but, as we have seen, immediate scheme realizations exist as well.

4.2.4 Threshold Elements

Consider now another interesting feature of the λ-structure.

Statement 9. *The digital compressor is a threshold element.*

It is known that a threshold element is an (n,1)-port network, behaving in accordance with the following formula:

$$f(x_1, x_2, ..., x_n) = \begin{cases} 1, & \text{if } \sum_{i=1}^{n} w_i x_i \geq T, \\ 0, & \text{if } \sum_{i=1}^{n} w_i x_i < T, \end{cases}$$

where $x_1, ..., x_n$ are binary signals at the inputs, $w_1, ..., w_n$ are the weights of corresponding inputs, and T is the threshold.

We shall consider the compressor inputs as the input ports of the threshold element, and the T-th compressor output as the output port.

Suppose that $w = 1$ $(i = 1, ..., n)$. Then, for any unitary code,

$$\sum_{i=1}^{n} w_i x_i = \sum_{i=1}^{n} x_i = Q_n^I.$$

By definition, the signal at the T-th compressor output is "1" if $Q_n^I \geq T$, and "0" in the contrary case. Hence, the compressor realizes the functions of the threshold element with the input weights $w_i = 1$.

Using different compressor outputs, one may set the threshold T in the range from 1 to n. Moreover, one can construct threshold elements with arbitrary weights of the inputs on the basis of a digital compressor, by means of supplementary input transformers (see, e.g., the "wired tree" above).

In the next Chapter we shall describe some arithmetic devices using λ-structures as main operational units.

CHAPTER 5

Solving Numerical Problems

5.1. *Binary Arithmetic Based on Vertical Processing*

We now consider the design of a *vertical pipeline adder*.
The algorithm of vertical addition consists in sequential calculation of the number of ones in the bit-slices of the initial array, beginning with the least significant digit. The partial sums obtained are summed, with the systematic shift of one position to the left, taking into account the weights of the ones in the processed bit-slices. This procedure has a pipeline character, which determines the structure of the processor and its name.

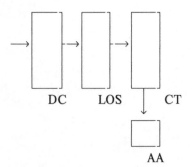

DC   LOS   CT

AA

Fig.5.1. Vertical pipeline adder.

The vertical pipeline adder (Fig.5.1.) consists of four units: a Digital Compressor (DC), a Leading Ones Selector (LOS), a Code

Transformer (CT), and an Adder-Accumulator (AA). The first three units perform the proper counting of the number of ones in the bit-slices (the weighting), and the last the addition of partial sums.

To realize weighting, the following technique is used here. At first, the compressor DC transforms the next bit-slice (unitary code) into the equivalent normalized unitary code (NUC). Then the selector LOS produces a signal marking the position of the first "one" of the NUC, that is, an equivalent unit positional code (UPC). Finally, the transformer CT outputs a binary number corresponding to the weight of the given bit-slice.

We have considered already several schemes of digital compressors. Note that in a vertical pipeline adder a pipeline compressor should be used.

The Leading Ones Selector is essentially a transformer (NUC→UPC), and can be realized as described in the previous Chapter. The last transformer (UPC→2) can be realized by means of a simple ROM, or as a table look-up transformer in an α-structure (see below).

The Adder-Accumulator needs no separate discussion. Observe only that it should ensure finishing of the shift and adding of the next partial sum in one cycle time. Then, the total time necessary to perform reductive summation in the device considered will depend only on the length n of the elements of the initial array. Taking into account the filling time n-1 of the pipeline compressor (the "depth" of the pipeline), it follows that the whole procedure time is approximately 2n steps.

Vertical multiplier. The multiplication procedure A x B, where A and B are n-bit binary integers, is none other than addition of an array of n partial products (i.e. shifted multiplicands A), under the control of bits of the multiplier B.

Suppose that the array of partial products is formed in the memory M1 (Fig.5.2). If a column of AND gates controlled by a multiplier is placed between the memory M1 and a vertical adder, and in such a scheme the reductive addition described above is performed, then the product C = A x B is obtained. The vertical adder must have, in this case, n inputs. The multiplication is made in 2n steps.

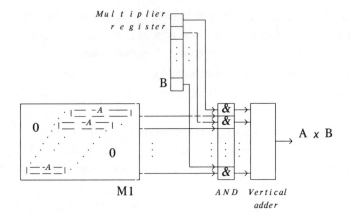

Fig.5.2. Vertical multiplier.

Inner product processor. The algorithm and scheme of vertical multiplication considered above can be applied to the case when the input array consists of n submatrices (n is the dimension of the vector arguments), so that the i-th submatrix corresponds to the partial products participating in generation of the product of the i-th components. Then, the scheme shown in Fig.5.3 will compute inner products.

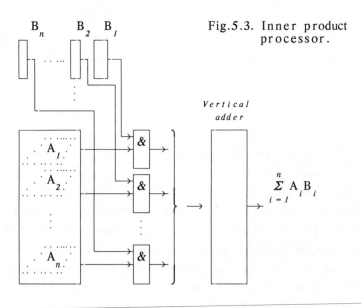

Fig.5.3. Inner product processor.

5.2. Table Look-Up Arithmetic Units

Tables are quite often used in everyday life: flight schedules, telephone directories, tables of logarithms. In computing, a table is essentially the same thing as a finite automaton, which produces at its outputs values of a function, when values of the arguments are fed to its inputs. Ideally, no computations are needed.

In the "input field" of the table automaton (Fig.5.4) are written the accepted values of the argument (or of the arguments, for

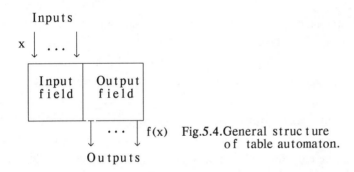

Fig.5.4. General structure of table automaton.

functions of several variables), and in the "output field" the corresponding values of the function. Such an automaton can be realized in any memory, so that the computation of a function reduces to a single memory access. This seems to be the fastest of possible computation techniques, and it would be tempting to replace all computations by table look-ups. In a sense, the development of computer science is advancing in this direction.

We will now consider some specific problems concerning the main obstacle met in table look-up: to achieve acceptable accuracy, a very high memory volume is required. Suppose we want to use the table look-up method for computing values of the function $f(x) = \sin x$ in the interval $[0, \pi/2]$. The table of sines may be prepared beforehand. To obtain accuracy, e.g., 2^{-16}, it is necessary in this instance to divide the interval into 2^{16} subintervals, and for each of these (more precisely, for one of its ends) to compute, with accuracy to the 16th binary digit, the corresponding values of $\sin x$. Now, if we write this table into the computer memory, and identify the values of the argument   x   with the order number of subintervals, then, to compute the sine, a single memory access suffices.

However, this would require an excessive memory volume:

$$M = 16*2^{16} = 2^{20} \text{ bit.}$$

There are different approaches to reducing memory expenditure in realizing table look-up computing. The most popular is diminishing the number of subintervals, and computation of corrections ensuring the required accuracy by means of some arithmetic unit. This is called the table-interpolation method. In the simplest case, linear interpolation is used, which requires two supplementary operations, one multiplication and one addition, for each value of the function. The argument   x   (n-digit binary number) is divided in two parts: the more significant   N   digits are considered as values of the argument in the nodes x_0 and used for address generation of corresponding interpolation coefficients in the table memory (in this case, coefficients are stored for 2^N uniformly distributed nodes); the less significant n-N   digits represent the increment of the argument on the given subinterval.

It is readily shown that supplementing table look-up by means of interpolation essentially reduces the memory expenditure, which becomes, for accuracy 2^{-n}, only $n*2^{n/2}$ bits.

For the preceding example (n = 16):

$$M' = 16*2^8 = 2^{12} \text{ bit.}$$

We assume up to this point uniform division of the interval, in which the errors in different subintervals may significantly vary. As the maximal error on the whole approximation interval is determined by the maximal of errors in all subintervals, the number of these has to be increased to diminish the error. That is why, the memory volume has to be unacceptably increased to achieve the required accuracy.

One can reduce the memory volume by equalizing errors in the subintervals. As a result, the interval of approximation is usually subdivided into unequal subinter,vals. In using such subdivision, the search of a subinterval becomes, for conventional memories, a rather troublesome problem. On the other hand, such a search is performed easily, as we know, in DF-structures realizing the search of adjacent numbers as the basic operation.

The structure of a specialized table look-up processor using these features is shown in Fig.5.5. The table storage consists here of two memory units: the memory M1 for the nodal values of the argument, and the memory M2 for interpolation coefficients. The argument x fed to the input register IR is compared simultaneously with all the nodal values, by means of a parallel comparator PC selecting the single subinterval corresponding to the given x. The output signal of the comparator is used for retrieval of interpolation coefficients from the coefficient memory M2.

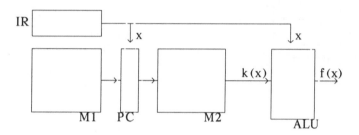

Fig.5.5. Table look-up processor.

It may be shown that for computation of elementary functions sin x, tg x, 2^x etc., due to the use of non-uniform subdivision, a 5 to 10 times memory economy is achieved, depending on the method of approximation.

Now consider the design procedure for some table look-up code transformers and arithmetic units based on an α-structure.

To design any coder, it is sufficient to write into the α-matrix the required table of encoding. When a signal $z = 1$ is fed to a row of this matrix, a code corresponding to the contents of this row appears at the outputs x' of the lower boundary. An example is represented in Fig.5.6., which shows an α-coder for binary coding of decimal

86

figures (transformer 10→BCD). To all inputs x,y of the upper boundary the constants "zero" are fed.

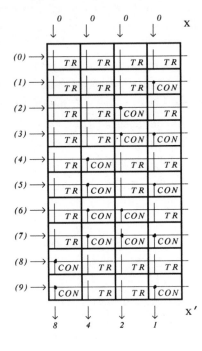

Fig.5.6. α-coder (transformer 10→BCD).

A useful feature of the α-coder is its flexibility and ease rearrangement: as the α-matrix can realize a reprogrammable PLA, changing the encoding tables is performed easily and fast.

It is known that every associative memory can perform the functions of a universal decoder. To do this, it suffices to write into the memory the required table of decoding. Then, when the word which has to be decoded is fed to the inputs of the associative memory as a comparand, the response signal appears at the single output corresponding to the given word. Hence, a decoder may be realized in an α-matrix operating as an associative memory (2α-matrix, see Chapter 4).

Fig.5.7 shows as an example an α-matrix implementing the transformation of binary-coded decimal digits into a unit positional code (BCD→UPC).

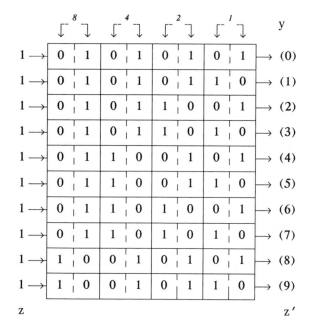

Fig.5.7. α-decoder (transformer BCD→UPC).

The simplicity of realization of coders and decoders allows us to implement table look-up arithmetic units in an α-structure. As an example, consider a design of a decimal adder (Fig.5.8) which represents the hardware implementation of the decimal addition table shown in Fig.5.9.

All the α-matrix is vertically divided into three fields: the field of decoders of summand combinations (A), the field of coders of sums (B), and the field of coders of the carry (C). In the first (uppermost) zone of the field of summand combinations is written the table of decoding of binary-decimal codes of the digits 0,1,...,9. In the second zone is a similar table for the digits 1,2,...,9, etc.

Though both inputs of the addition table are of equal value, the adder is designed, to save hardware, so that the larger of the two summands is fed to the inputs z (in the code "1 of 10"), and the lesser to the inputs x,y of the field of decoders (in the two-phase code "8-4-2-1").

The fields of the coders of sum and carry contain tables of coding sums and carries, for all summand combinations, according to the addition table.

88

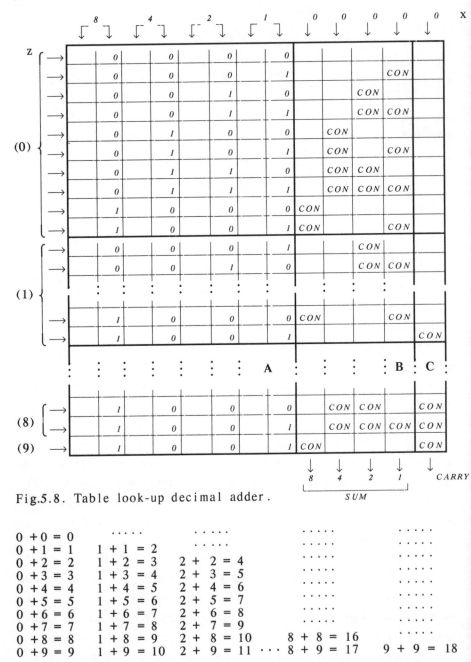

Fig.5.8. Table look-up decimal adder.

0 + 0 = 0   ....
0 + 1 = 1   1 + 1 = 2   ....
0 + 2 = 2   1 + 2 = 3   2 + 2 = 4   ....
0 + 3 = 3   1 + 3 = 4   2 + 3 = 5   ....
0 + 4 = 4   1 + 4 = 5   2 + 4 = 6   ....
0 + 5 = 5   1 + 5 = 6   2 + 5 = 7   ....
0 + 6 = 6   1 + 6 = 7   2 + 6 = 8   ....
0 + 7 = 7   1 + 7 = 8   2 + 7 = 9   ....
0 + 8 = 8   1 + 8 = 9   2 + 8 = 10   8 + 8 = 16   .....
0 + 9 = 9   1 + 9 = 10   2 + 9 = 11 ··· 8 + 9 = 17   9 + 9 = 18

Fig.5.9. Addition table.

The adder operates as follows. When the summands are fed to the inputs of the α-matrix, for each pair of summands there is a single row corresponding to that pair such that at the outputs of the field of decoders appears the signal $z' = 1$. This signal passes further along this row through the corresponding fields of coders, and causes the appearance of suitable values of the sum (in the code "8-4-2-1") and the carry at the outputs x' of the lower boundary of corresponding fields.

A decimal multiplier can be designed similarly. The decoders of the argument combinations should be the same as in the preceding scheme. Instead of coders of carry are coders of the high-order digit of the product. All coders are set according to the common multiplication table.

As the input decoders of the table look-up adder and multiplier are essentially the same, it is appropriate in practice to overlap both devices so that one unit performs simultaneously (or alternatively) both operations, addition and multiplication.

5.3. *Arithmetic Computations in Unitary Codes*

The properties of compressors we have considered allow us to construct arithmetic devices for unitarily-coded number systems.

In Fig.5.10 the structure of an adder for a Unitarily-Coded Decimal (UCD) system is shown. In this case, the compressor has to have 19 inputs (two groups of nine inputs each for the unitary codes of the summands A and B, and one extra input for carry c_i from the preceding lower digit), and, correspondingly, 19 outputs.

The compressor DC produces at its outputs, as is readily seen, a normalized unitary code corresponding to the total number of "ones" fed to its inputs, that is, to the sum of digits of the summands A and B, and the carry c_i. At the same time, it produces (acting as a threshold element) at its 10th output the carry signal c_{i+1} into the following position. According to the rules of decimal addition, if $A + B < 10$, then the digit of the processed position is $S = A + B$. In this case, $c_{i+1} = 0$ and at the inputs of the AND gate group G1 there

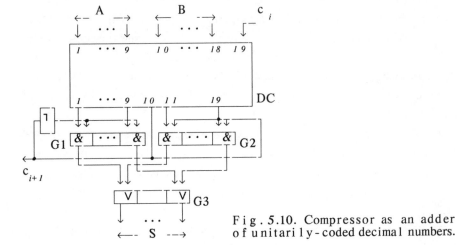

Fig. 5.10. Compressor as an adder of unitarily-coded decimal numbers.

is an enable signal which transmits the correct value of the sum from the outputs 1...9 of the compressor to the outputs of the OR gate group G3. If, however, $A + B \geq 10$, then $S = (A+B)-10$. In this case, $c_{i+1} = 1$, all the gates of the AND group G1 become closed while the gates G2 become open, so that the correct value of the sum S is transmitted to the outputs of the OR group G3 from the outputs 11...19 of the compressor.

Thus, an n-digit parallel UCD adder may be built as a chain of one-digit adders.

Unitary subtraction is realized quite simply. In Fig.5.11.a is shown a scheme of an n-bit subtractor of normalized unitary codes, and in Fig.5.11.b an example of subtraction (9-5=4). To obtain finally the difference in the normalized code, it is necessary to perform a concluding shift.

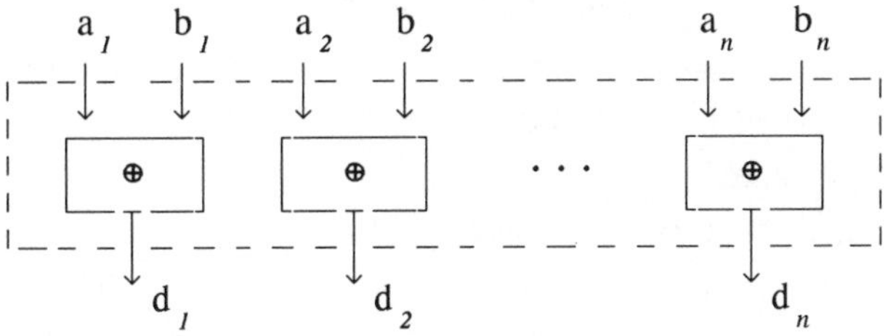

a)

A	1 1 1 1 1 1 1 1 1 0 0 0 0 0 0 0	(9)	
B	1 1 1 1 1 0 0 0 0 0 0 0 0 0 0 0	(5)	
D	0 0 0 0 0 1 1 1 1 0 0 0 0 0 0 0	(4)	b)

Fig.5.11. Subtraction in normalized unitary codes: a) sheme of subtractor; b) example of subtraction.

5.4. Arithmetic Units in Residue Number Systems

Basic definitions

We begin with fundamental notions concerning residue number systems [1].

Suppose a sequence $p_1, p_2, ..., p_n$ of positive integers is given, called henceforth system bases. The residue number system is a system in which a positive integer N is represented by the set of its residues (least remainders) upon the chosen bases:

$$N = (\alpha_1, \alpha_2, ..., \alpha_n),$$

so that each of the α_i, called *digits of* N, is obtained as follows:

$$\alpha_i = N - [N/p_i] \, p_i^{*)} \quad \text{(for i=1,2,...,n)};$$

that is, the i-th digit α_i of the number N is the least non-negative remainder of division of N by p_i.

---
*) ([x] denotes the integral part of the number x).

In contrast to positional systems, the computation of each digit is performed independently of other digits. Clearly, $0 \leq \alpha_i < p_i$.

As is known from number theory, if the numbers p_i are relatively prime, any non-negative integer $N \leq P = p_1 \ldots p_n$ is uniquely determined by its figures α_i.

Thus, the numbers from the range $0,1,2,\ldots,P-1$ can be represented by these figures. This is called representation in *residue number system* (RNS). As for positional systems, the range of representable numbers grows with n as the product of bases, whereas the digit capacity necessary to represent the numbers of the range grows as the sum of the digit capacities of the bases.

Consider the rules of addition and multiplication in a residue number system when both operands, as well as the result, are in the range $[0,P)$.

Let the operands A and B be represented by residues α_i and β_i, respectively, in the bases p_i $(i=1,2,\ldots,n)$. The results of addition and multiplication $A + B$ and AB are then represented by residues γ_i and δ_i, respectively, in the same system of bases:

$$A = (\alpha_1, \alpha_2, \ldots, \alpha_n),$$
$$B = (\beta_1, \beta_2, \ldots, \beta_n),$$
$$A+B = (\gamma_1, \gamma_2, \ldots, \gamma_n),$$
$$AB = (\delta_1, \delta_2, \ldots, \delta_n).$$

Here the relations $A < P$, $B < P$, $A+B < P$, $AB < P$ hold.

It is readily seen that γ is congruent with $\alpha_i + \beta_i \pmod{p_i}$, and δ_i is congruent with $\alpha_i \beta_i \pmod{p_i}$; that is,

$$\gamma_i \equiv \alpha_i + \beta_i \pmod{p_i},$$
$$\delta_i \equiv \alpha_i \beta_i \pmod{p_i}.$$

As digits of the result are taken, correspondingly,

$$\gamma_i = \alpha_i + \beta_i - [(\alpha_i + \beta_i)/p_i]p_i,$$
$$\delta_i = \alpha_i \beta_i [\alpha_i \beta_i / p_i]p_i.$$

Examples of addition and multiplication in the residue number system are given below.

Let the bases of the system be: $p_1=3$, $p_2=5$, $p_3=7$; the range of representation is given by $P = p_1 p_2 p_3 = 105$.

Example 1. Add $A = 17$ and $B = 63$.

In the chosen bases, these numbers are represented as

$$A = 17 = (2,2,3), \quad B = 63 = (0,3,0).$$

In accordance with the above addition rule, we obtain

$$A + B = (2,0,3).$$

It is readily verified that the number $(2,0,3)$ is 80 and equals the sum of the operands A and B.

Example 2. Multiply $A = 17$ and $B = 6$.

In the chosen bases, these numbers are represented as

$$A = 17 = (2,2,3), \quad B = 6 = (0,1,6).$$

In accordance with the above multiplication rule, we obtain

$$AB = (0,2,4).$$

It is readily verified that the number $(0,2,4)$ is 102 and equals to the product of the operands A and B.

Residue number systems have some advantages and shortcomings in arithmetic computations, which will be now outlined.

The main advantages are: independence of figures and the possibility of their separate concurrent processing; small digit capacities of residues, for bases needed in practice, which allows us to use table arithmetic.

The shortcomings are: impossibility of visual comparison of numbers, as the representation of a number does not give any impression of its value; absence of simple tests of overflow, that is for obtaining results out of the range $[0,P)$; the limitation of the system to non-negative integers.

Structure of arithmetic unit

Fig.5.12 shows the general structure of an arithmetic unit in a residue number system. Note that such a structure is applicable to an arbitrary number system: the input transformer of arguments - the operational unit in the given number system - the output transformer of results.

The specific property of the arithmetic unit in a residue number system that we shall describe below is wide use of parallel processing and specialized DF-structures.

One of the main blocks of the arithmetic unit in a residue number system is (mod m) adder. Therefore we now consider variants of designing such adders in distributed structures.

The (mod m) adder has evidently to perform addition (mod m) of two numbers, a and b: $c \equiv a+b$ (mod m), where a,b,c are changing in the interval [0,m-1].

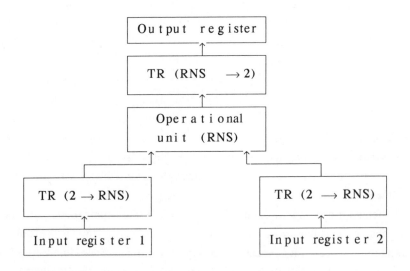

Fig.5.12. Arithmetic unit in residue number system.

If a,b,c are binary-coded numbers, then for construction of a (mod m) adder conventional binary adders may be used, supplemented by feedbacks corresponding to the given module m. In Fig.5.13. an example is shown of a scheme of a (mod 5) adder In this figure Σ denotes a full binary adder. When feedbacks are absent, the three-stage binary adder performs addition (mod 8). Due to feedbacks 1

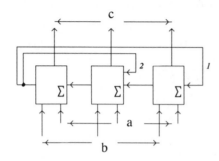

Fig.5.13. (mod 5) adder based on full binary adders.

and 2, at overflow the correction "-3" is introduced, and the module of the adder is diminished to 5. If, for instance, the feedback 2 were deleted, then only the correction "-1" is left, so that the scheme becomes (mod 7) adder.

Homogeneous (mod m) adders

Consider now the case when a,b,c are coded in a unit positional code (UPC). For instance, for m = 5: 0 - 10000, 1 - 01000, 2 - 00100, 3 - 00010, 4 - 00001.

For this coding, the operation of a (mod 5) adder is described by the truth table shown in Fig.5.14. According to this table, the (mod 5) adder may be realized by means of five logical functions of ten variables.

Note an interesting feature of addition (mod m) in UPC. The sum (c) is obtained by cyclic shift of the unit in the code of the first summand (a) on b positions to the right ($0 \leq b \leq$ m-1). This feature is readily verified by means of the truth table (Fig.5.14). If, for instance, b = 2 (00100), a = 1 (01000), then c = 3 (00010), which corresponds to the shift of the unit in the code of a on two positions to the right; if b = 4 (00001), a = 2 (00100), then c = 1 (01000), which corresponds to the cyclic shift of the unit in the code of a on four positions to the right.

a					b					c				
a_0	a_1	a_2	a_3	a_4	b_0	b_1	b_2	b_3	b_4	c_0	c_1	c_2	c_3	c_4
1	0	0	0	0	1	0	0	0	0	1	0	0	0	0
0	1	0	0	0	1	0	0	0	0	0	1	0	0	0
0	0	1	0	0	1	0	0	0	0	0	0	1	0	0
0	0	0	1	0	1	0	0	0	0	0	0	0	1	0
0	0	0	0	1	1	0	0	0	0	0	0	0	0	1
1	0	0	0	0	0	1	0	0	0	0	1	0	0	0
0	1	0	0	0	0	1	0	0	0	0	0	1	0	0
0	0	1	0	0	0	1	0	0	0	0	0	0	1	0
0	0	0	1	0	0	1	0	0	0	0	0	0	0	1
0	0	0	0	1	0	1	0	0	0	1	0	0	0	0
1	0	0	0	0	0	0	1	0	0	0	0	1	0	0
0	1	0	0	0	0	0	1	0	0	0	0	0	1	0
0	0	1	0	0	0	0	1	0	0	0	0	0	0	1
0	0	0	1	0	0	0	1	0	0	1	0	0	0	0
0	0	0	0	1	0	0	1	0	0	0	1	0	0	0
1	0	0	0	0	0	0	0	1	0	0	0	0	1	0
0	1	0	0	0	0	0	0	1	0	0	0	0	0	1
0	0	1	0	0	0	0	0	1	0	1	0	0	0	0
0	0	0	1	0	0	0	0	1	0	0	1	0	0	0
0	0	0	0	1	0	0	0	1	0	0	0	1	0	0
1	0	0	0	0	0	0	0	0	1	0	0	0	0	1
0	1	0	0	0	0	0	0	0	1	1	0	0	0	0
0	0	1	0	0	0	0	0	0	1	0	1	0	0	0
0	0	0	1	0	0	0	0	0	1	0	0	1	0	0
0	0	0	0	1	0	0	0	0	1	0	0	0	1	0

Fig. 5.14. Truth table of (mod 5) addition.

This property allows us to represent the scheme of the (mod m) adder as a regular structure.

Exploiting the same feature, one can build a universal (mod m) adder as a two-dimensional iterative circuit; to do this one needs, however, to represent one of the summands in the unitary code.

In Fig.5.15 the scheme of a homogeneous (mod 3) adder is shown. Each cell realizes the functions: $x' = z \lor xy$, $z' = xy$. The output z' of the last cell of each row is connected to the input z of the first cell in the same row (cyclic closure). One of the summands is fed to the inputs x of the upper row in UPC, and the second to the buses y in the unitary code.

In any row where y = 0, all the z are zero, hence, x′= x, so that the data coming to this row are not shifted. If, however, y = 1, then z′= x, and x′= z, so that the variable x coming to the input of any cell is routed to the output x′ of the right neighbouring cell. In such a cell, a shift on one position to the right is performed. The whole (cyclic) shift performed by this scheme corresponds to the number of "ones" fed to the buses y,

that is to the value of the second summand. Hence, at the outputs x′ of the bottom row the (mod 3) sum is produced.

The scheme for any module is built similarly. Note that the arrangement of "ones" in the unitary code is arbitrary, provided that the total number of "ones" Q_n^I corresponds to the value of the summand. By the same reason, this device can operate with an arbitrary number of rows exceeding m. As to the number of columns, this has to be exactly m, to ensure the required cycle length.

The scheme just considered, with a fixed cycle length, is clearly inconvenient. It is desirable to have the flexibility to set the device on various cycles, to allow it to be used for various m.

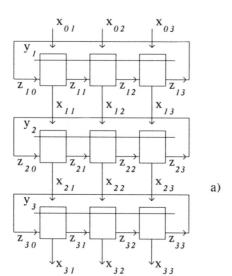

a)

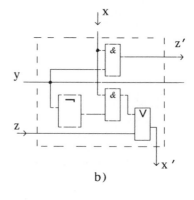

b)

Fig.5.15. Homogeneous (mod 3) adder: a) general structure; b) logic circuit of a cell.

98

Fig.5.16 shows the scheme of a homogeneous rearrangeable (mod m) adder. Compared with the scheme in Fig.5.15, here a vertical control bus t is introduced in every column, and in every row a horizontal channel v realizing the function $v' = v \vee xyt$. The output v' of the first cell of each row is connected to the input z of the same cell. To the inputs v of the right boundary the constants $v_0 = 0$ are fed. The coding of the summands and the sum is the same as in the previous scheme.

We now show that if the matrix has size m x m, then it can be set on arbitrary modules n ≤ m.

Put the control signal t = 1 to the bus t of the n-th column. As a result, in all the cells of this column $v' = xy = z'$; that is, the output z' of the n-th cell of each row is switched into the channel v, is routed to the left along this channel (as in all other cells $v' = v$), and, finally, in the first cell of each row, is connected to the input z. This clearly corresponds to the setting of the device onto the cycle length n.

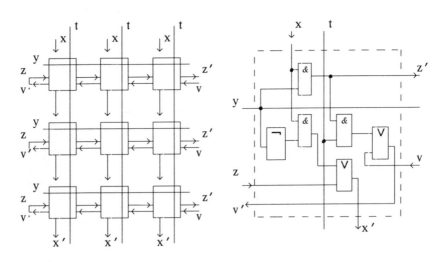

Fig.5.16. Rearrangeable homogeneous (mod m) adder.

The schemes in Fig.5.15 and Fig.5.16 are of interest here as devices realizing (mod m) addition. However, they may find broader application, as each of them is essentially a binary shifter.

Transformer 2→RNS

As was said above, the transformation 2→RNS consists in computation of n residues $(\bmod\ p_i)$ $(i = 1,...,n)$ for all bases of the chosen system. It was mentioned that independent processing of separate figures is possible. Therefore, in the arithmetic unit n similar paths (according to the number of bases) operating independently and in parallel can be organized.

Thus, the transformer 2→RNS contains n independent units of *residue calculators* (RC), computing simultaneously the residues upon all the bases p_i (Fig.5.17).

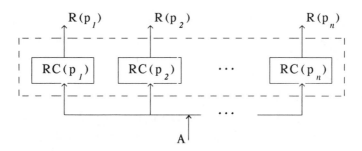

Fig.5.17. Transformer 2→RNS (general structure).

Consider a possible design of a residue calculator.

It is known that the (mod m) residue of an n-bit binary integer N is

$$R(N) \equiv \sum_{i=0}^{n-1} \alpha_i 2^i \ (\bmod\ m) \equiv \sum_{i=0}^{n-1} \alpha_i c_i \ (\bmod\ m),$$

where $\alpha_i = 0$ or 1, $c_i \equiv 2^i (\bmod\ m)$, $0 \le c_i < m$.

It is known also that the sequence of residues c_i of the powers of a positional base is periodic. Denote the length of its period k. Then all the positions of the initial number N can be divided into k disjoint groups, each containing all positions with the same value of c_i. For some modules m the initial segment s_{IN} (preceding the first period) can exist. Each of k groups contains n/k positions of

the   initial   number.   If   the   last   period   is   incomplete,   the
corresponding groups are supplemented by zeros.

Dependent on the distribution of the coefficients α_i, each group
will contain a certain number ω of ones. Call *partial residue*
(mod m) of the j-th group (j = 1,...,k) the value

$$R_j = \omega_j c_j \ (\text{mod } m),$$

where ω_j is the number of ones in the j-th group, and c_j is the
weight of each "one" of the corresponding group.

Then,

$$R(N) \equiv [\sum_{j-1}^{k} R_j + s_{IN}] (\text{mod } m).$$

Now, the problem reduces to computation of partial residues for each
group of digits of equal weights, and to consequent addition (mod m)
of these residues.

Consider the scheme of a transformer 2→RNS, for the specific case:
n = 32, m = 5 (Fig.5.18).

In this case the sequence of residues has period   k = 4. c_1 = 1,
c_2 = 2, c_3 = 4, c_4 = 3. The initial segment is absent. The positions of
the initial number are divided into four groups, with eight digits in
each   (to illustrate this, in Fig.5.18 every position is marked by its
weight). The partial residues for each group are computed by a
particular set of units   "Digital   Compressor (DC) - TRansformer
NUC→UPC (TR) - Partial residue Coder (PC)". Then the chain of (mod 5)
adders Σ sums the partial residues of all the groups. As the
initial segment s_{IN} is now absent (so its weight is taken as zero) the
UPC of zero (10000) is fed to the inputs of the first (mod 5) adder.
The operation of all units of this device, with the exception of the
residue coder, is clear from the preceding.

Consider now the design of the residue coder. The UPC of the output
of each transformer TR corresponds to the number of ones in the
current eight-bit group. The partial residues (mod 5), dependent on
the number of ones in a group ω_j and the "weight" of each "one" of the
group c_j, are shown in Table 5.1.

Using this table, the residue coder can easily be designed, for example, on the basis of an α-structure.

Similar rules of building partial residues are true for arbitrary n and m. This allows us to design the required residue coder for any specific case. A unified homogeneous coder rearrangeable according to given n and m is also readily designed.

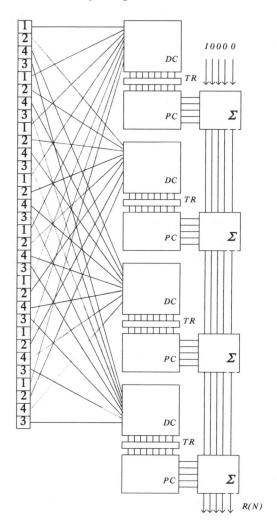

Fig.5.18. Transformer 2-RNS based on digital compressors.

Note that division of the positions of the initial binary number allows us to reduce the expenditure on hardware, and, at the same time, to gain in performance, due to parallel computing of all partial residues.

Table 5.1

	1	2	3	4	5	6	7	8	ω_j
1	1	2	3	4	0	1	2	3	
2	2	4	1	3	0	2	4	1	
4	4	3	2	1	0	4	3	2	$\leftarrow R_j$
3	3	1	4	2	0	3	1	4	

c_j

Operational unit

In accordance with the established rules, realization of the arithmetic operations of addition and multiplication in a residue number system reduces to parallel independent performing of n operations (corr., + or x) over the figures of the operands, for all bases p_i. Therefore the operational unit of the arithmetic device has to contain n identical schemes of adders or multipliers, see Fig.5.19.

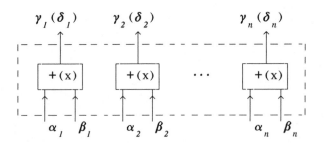

Fig.5.19. Structure of the operational unit.

If UPC coding is used inside the arithmetic device, as we assumed above, then the residue adders are naturally built according to the to the standard scheme, as in other units of the device (for instance, as in Fig.5.16).

Table 5.2

	1	2	3	4	5	6	7	8	9	10	$\leftarrow \alpha_i$
1	1										
2	2	4					$\gamma_i = \alpha_i * \beta_i$				
3	3	6	9								
4	4	8	1	5							
5	5	10	4	9	3						
6	6	1	7	2	8	3					
7	7	3	10	6	2	9	5				
8	8	5	2	10	7	4	1	9			
9	9	7	5	3	1	10	8	6	4		
0	10	9	8	7	6	5	4	3	2	1	

$\uparrow$
β_i

To build multipliers, it is appropriate to apply table look-up methods. Table 5.2 shows an example of a multiplication table in RNS for p = 11. It is evident that such a table can be realized in an α-matrix similarly to the binary-decimal units considered above.

CHAPTER 6

Non-Numerical Data Processing

6.1. Features of Non-Numerical Problems

Throughout its history, computing technique has been developed as a means of automatization of *computations*. At the same time it has always been necessary to solve problems of a non-numerical character. In principle, general purpose computers can solve these problems, but their efficiency is often not satisfactory.

We pay particular attention to non-numerical processing, since non-numerical data handling is of special and increasing importance. For instance, in developing modern computing systems, the methods of artificial intelligence are essential, and these, as a rule, require processing of extensive arrays of non-numerical data.

Some specialists believe that in the near future *computations* will be largely replaced, in general, by *searches* in databases, hypertext systems, knowledge bases, expert systems and logical inference systems. It is now considered that for the successful solution of AI problems computer power should be increased by 3 or 4 orders.

An analysis of various applications of non-numerical processing leads to the following classification:

- problems of data retrieval (simple and complicated associative searches);
- set-theoretical operations on data arrays;

- special operations on data arrays (elimination of duplicates, recoding, etc.);
- special operations of relational algebra;
- symbol processing;
- processing of list structures;
- graph problems.

Non-numerical processing also includes problems of commutation and transformation of data structures (permutation, sorting, transposition, etc.), which we discuss in the next Chapter.

Characteristic features of non-numerical problems are:

* very large size of processed arrays (tens and hundreds of megabytes);

* organization of data in the form of definite structures: tables, lists, graphs, etc.;

* use of non-arithmetic operations: the basic processing consists in retrieval of relevant data, comparison, editing, transformation of data structures, etc.;

* regular structure of the data: the processed arrays contain a large number of identical elements; all "records" in large data arrays and databases are organized in the same way; the relations in relational data models consist of tuples of the same type (note that such a structure of arrays provides for easy implementation of parallel processing);

* high requirements on time characteristics: many of the problems of non-numerical processing have to be solved in real time; large data systems require concurrent maintenance of numerous users; operation with databases in interactive mode requires fast response.

General purpose computers are oriented mainly towards computational algorithms. They are hardly ever suited for processing of complicated data structures.

There is an evident need for specialized hardware for non-numerical processing; this need has been recognized by specialists for a long time. We go on to a short review of research in the field of non-numerical processors; then we shall describe some algorithms and devices for non-numerical processing based on implementation of DF-structures.

The first problems of this class which got hardware support were those of data retrieval. As early as the middle of the 50s, Content-Addressed Memories (CAM) were proposed (see Chapter 3). The basic operation of a CAM is the equality search. One of the arguments of this operation is an array, and the second a scalar (comparand).

In the 60s, a variety of associative array processors were developed, intended for searches upon manifold criteria, and for ordered retrieval of data. Operation of all these processors was founded on multiple use of the basic operation "equality search". The result of this operation is a logical vector picking out the rows of the CAM containing appropriate elements, by its "ones". By means of this basic operation, microprograms realizing more complicated searches, orderings, and other procedures may be constructed.

Nevertheless, the practical use of hardware means advanced slowly, mainly because the technology of the time hampered realization of complicated specialized devices.

6.2. Database Machines

Of particular importance for the development of non-numerical processors has been the conception of relational databases, suggested by Codd in 1970 [14]. This conception led to the definition of an important class of data processing problems described by operations of relational algebra and α-expressions of relational calculus. In addition, the relational model, due to its inherent parallelism, homogeneity, and massiveness, is appropriate for parallel hardware implementation, and is well suited for the technique of associative processing.

The necessity to provide high performance of associative processing and the search for new architectures led, in the 70s, to development of a number of projects of specialized non-numerical processors, oriented towards the problems of relational databases: CAFS, CASSM, RARES, DBC, etc. Most of these were based on the idea of large-capacity rotating memory with "head-per-track", first suggested by Slotnick in 1970 [72], as an alternative to the expensive content-addressed memory with distributed logic. Such a massive parallel processing technique we call *quasi-associative* or *vertical.* Detailed description of various quasi-associative processors may be found in Ozkarahan's book [62].

Quasi-associative processors allow efficient parallel associative searches in large data arrays. Parallel realization of these operations provides improvement in performance sufficient only for relatively simple queries. For more complicated problems, these processors are not efficient. Examples of such problems are: intersection of arrays, join, deletion of duplicates in projection.

Comparative analysis of the performance of some of these non-numerical processors (see, for example, [38]) showed that they increase performance by 5-10 times for simple queries, compared with program implementation of the same queries on general purpose computers, whereas for complicated queries the increase in performance is negligible. The experience achieved in designing and testing of these processors showed that a unified approach reducing all problems to sequences of associative searches cannot ensure good results.

Further development of non-numerical computers required a differentiated approach to the hardware support of problems of different complexity, deeper use of parallelism and the application of more sophisticated hardware solutions.

Numerous projected database machines (DBMs) have now been designed and described. Some of them have been manufactured and have appeared on the market. We shall discuss some typical DBMs, beginning with related classification principles.

6.2.1. *Classification of DBMs*

Generally speaking, one could apply here the widely known classification schemes, e.g. that of Flynn or of Haendler, which are essentially universal. However, such specialized computers as DBMs have important specific features not represented by universal classifications. Therefore we need here some more detailed scheme.

According to Hsiao [47], three categories of DBMs may be distinguished, related to their technology and practical availability:

1. "Now" machines, for which both hardware and software are available at present.

2. "Approaching" machines, which become real as appropriate technology (both software and hardware) matures.

3. "Future" machines, depending on the appearance of new technologies, as yet absent. Hsiao thinks that one of these could be a DBM using associative memories of gigabyte capacity.

Any DBM is a complicated hardware/software system, the general architecture of which depends on distribution of its functions between hardware and software. From this viewpoint, five variants are considered by Hsiao.

1. The conventional approach to database management: the whole Database Management System (DBMS) software, as well as I/O control, is realized in a general purpose computer. The database processors (back-end processors) relieve the host computer from database and input/output control. They realize this by means of special software and/or hardware. *Software back-end processors* and *hardware back-end processors* are distinguished.

2. Systems using *one* software back-end processor. It may be any standard general purpose computer with appropriate characteristics. No modifications in hardware are necessary. Note that such a peripheral processor can support several host machines in time-sharing mode.

3. If significant improvement in performance is necessary, for large database and considerable query flow, *several* such software back-end processors working in parallel can be used.

4. Systems using *"intelligent controllers"*. Here some elements of microprogram and hardware support appear. In this case, the back-end processor is built from standard computing elements, but its hardware architecture is specially oriented towards efficient implementation of the DBMS functions. The intelligent controller has its own instruction set. Usually some preprocessing of queries in the host machine is assumed, where they are translated into the instruction set of the back-end processor. Accordingly, after obtaining of necessary data from the back-end processor, the host machine arranges the final result and outputs it to the user.

The database machine IDM-500, to be described below, is an example of an intelligent controller.

5. Systems using *hardware back-ends*. These differ from all the preceding by significant changes in hardware architecture, e.g. by the use of parallel associative processors, specialized interconnection networks, filters, hardware sorters, etc.

Boral and Redfield [11] proposed a system of morphological taxonomy of DBMs, allowing a rather compact description and classification. Their system uses seven main characteristics, cited below.

1. *Functions*. This characteristic shows what part of the whole work of DBMS is delegated to the DBM. The following variants are possible: DBM is used only to improve access to the database; DBM implements some individual operations of relational algebra; DBM realizes the whole query tree in a unified process.

2. *Number of concurrently implemented functions*: one, several, many.

3. *Type of concurrency* of various stages of implementation of a single function. Possible variants: no concurrency; parallel processing; pipeline processing; parallel/pipeline processing.

4. *Basic method* used in realization of functions. A broad range of methods is possible, beginning with program implementation in a computer of von Neumann type (e.g., algorithms with nested cycles), up to specialized hardware devices implementing operations of relational algebra by means of hash coding, sorting, etc.

5. *Interaction with external memories*. Characterizes existence and capacity of buffer memory in a DBM, as well as the method of staging data from an external memory.

6. *Method of associative access*: use of filters, indexes, pointers etc.

7. *Organization of storage of databases*. The database can be stored in the external memory in the form of unordered normalized relations; of relations segmented upon the values of one attribute, or of several attributes. Storage may be based on domains or attributes with attached tuple identifiers, etc.

6.2.2. *IDM-500*

Consider as an example the commercial database machine *IDM-500* (Intelligent Database Machine) of Britton-Lee Corporation [48]. According to the Hsiao classification, it is a now-machine, belonging to the category of intelligent controllers.

The IDM-500 is a portable machine of size 25x60x30 cm, containing from 5 to 16 boards. Fig.6.1 shows the general structure of the IDM-500. The minimal set of the machine is of 5 boards:

1. Database processor - the main unit of the machine. This is a specialized microprogrammed processor implementing most of the system software functions and controlling all the resources of the system.

2. Channel I/O processor, realizing a sequential asynchronous or parallel (multiplexed) interface with 8 terminals or host computers. Up to 8 I/O processors are allowed.

3. Main memory of 256K bytes. Intended for buffering data blocks coming from the discs. Stores also programs and data needed for execution of queries. Connection of up to 12 memory blocks is permitted (i.e., enlarging of memory up to 3 Mbytes).

4. Disc controller, transferring data between the external memories and the main memory of the IDM-500. Controls from 1 to 4 magnetic tape units. From 1 to 4 disc controllers can be used in the system.

5. Memory control and synchronization device. Controls the memory system. Realizes error detection and correction. Ensures high-speed pipelined data transfer needed in using an additional board - a database accelerator.

As indicated in the literature [38], the IDM-500 speeds up database management about 10 times compared to a software-implemented DBMS. Besides, it relieves the host computer from this task.

Further improvement of the IDM-500 can be achieved by means of an additional super-high-speed specialized processor mounted on a single board, called a *database accelerator* (DBA). This processor has a special instruction set designed to support relational databases. Each instruction is accomplished in 100 ns. The DBA can initiate magnetic discs and perform preprocessing, for instance, "on-the-fly" filtering

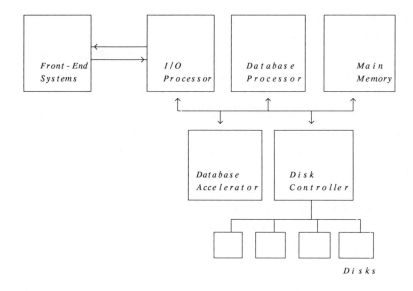

Fig.6.1. General structure of IDM-500.

in the process of transferring data from discs into the main memory. When there is a DBA, most of the hard tasks are delegated from the main database processor to the DBA, which performs them much faster. The DBA uses a pipeline processor with performance of 10 Mips. It is built from standard integrated circuits, and its cost is only twice that of a similar board containing a standard microcomputer. At the same time, it gives a 30-times speedup compared to a general purpose computer, while realizing its special functions.

6.2.3. Delta

Now we describe shortly a specialized hardware system - the Japanese database machine *Delta* [70], which was developed within Japan's Fifth Generation Computer Project, and was intended as a software development tool.

Delta is one of the most complicated computers of this class. It has a quite sophisticated architecture and a very high level of hardware support; it ensures implementation of a wide set of instructions of different types: operations of relational algebra, arithmetic operations, aggregate functions, etc.

The main principle of performing operations of relational algebra is the pipelined-stream processing of ordered chains of attributes.

The Fig.6.2 shows the general structure of the Delta computer.

The Interface Processor (IP) is necessary for flexible interaction with multiple users (in accordance with the main destination of the system), and for isolation of other subsystems from tasks concerning query analysis and correction of user's errors.

The Main Controller (MC) coordinates the operation of all subsystems and performs the main part of system functions (compiling of instructions, security, integrity, recovery, etc.). The Main Controller is a general purpose computer.

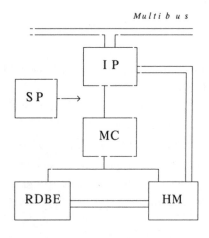

Fig. 6.2. The structure of Delta computer.

The complexity of the system and high reliability requirements called for a separate Service Processor (SP) connected with all subsystems, which gets and processes error massages and performs all the subsidiary programs.

The main work-load in the Delta system is entrusted to the so-called Relational Database Engine (RDBE). Special attention was paid to the development of the structure and the algorithms of this subsystem. The main requirements to this machine are:

- implementation of a large set of DBMS functions;
- operation in pipelined-stream mode;
- processing "on-the-fly" at one run of data stream;
- regular structure oriented at VLSI implementation.

The operation of the Relational Database Engine is based on the merge-sort algorithm. As a rule, for two-way merge two FIFO queues are used, formed of preordered chains of elements. The merge processor compares the "top" elements of these chains, outputs the lesser of them into the output chain (assuming ascending ordering), and pushes the corresponding chain at one step.

Modifications of this algorithm allow implementation in the pipeline mode of a wide range of logical operations, including those of relational algebra. The main point of these modifications consists in changing the rules of chain formation, of comparison, and of pushing the next-in-turn elements. The rules are sufficiently simple, and are determined unambiguously by the contexts of the specific operations.

The Delta system pays much attention to the Hierarchical Memory (HM) subsystem. To supply the high-performance Relational Database Engine with a continuous data flow, the memory subsystem has to be organized in a proper way. There are two memory levels: the standard discs of total capacity up to 20 Gbytes, and the power-independent electronic disc of capacity up to 128 Mbytes.

In the Delta system an inner database scheme is used, based on storage of attributes with tuple identifiers, and a two-level clusterization (based upon the values of attributes and of identifiers).

To control the Hierarchical Memory subsystem a special controller is used (a general purpose computer). Its functions are:
- staging of data from the external memories into the electronic disc;
- cluster search;
- preparing of data streams for the Relational Engine;
- transferring of input streams into the Relational Engine and reception of resulting streams;
- transformation of attributes into tuples and vice versa;

- dumping of electronic disc contents at interruptions of power supply.

There are many different views on the choice of DBM architecture.

Ozkarahan is of the opinion that DBM architecture has to be developed in the direction of creating a "universal" non-numerical processor, which he calls GPN^2C (General Purpose Non-Numerical Computer) [62]. Such a machine must support: a) all the popular data models; b) full text searches and retrievals; c) operation of distributed databases, etc.

Hawthorn at al. are essentially of opposite opinion [38]. They think that the immediate needs of users should be studied. All users should be divided into type categories depending on application areas, database volume, frequency and character of queries. For each category a computer of corresponding complexity and cost should be proposed. An example of a computer for the "medium" category of users is the IDM-500.

In [37] Hawthorn showed undeniably that an "ideal" database machine satisfying all possible users cannot be designed.

We share this last viewpoint. Striving to universality, to unification of many different applications in a single computer, does not apparently conform to the modern outlook in digital systems architecture. It is more appropriate to develop a modular family of machines for non-numerical processing. Different machines of this family need to be designed with various combinations of modules, beginning with simple filters for selection "on-the-fly", up to complicated systems supporting all the functions of a relational DBMS. Choice of architecture should be such that maximal performance for a given specific application, at allowable expense, could be achieved.

An example of such modular architecture, using parallel homogeneous processors will be considered below.

An important feature of algorithms of associative and vertical processing, as well as of the hardware realizing them, is the use of *Binary Label Vectors* (BLV). The contents of the response register of an associative memory is just a BLV indicating by its "ones" the chosen words. The resulting signals on the boundaries of various DF-structures form label vectors. The mask register M in an associative module of the STARAN system is an BLV indicating active channels of the module.

Binary label vectors are widely used in the machine RAP (Relational Associative Processor) developed at Arizona State University under the direction of Ozkarahan [62]. The main data storage structure in this machine is the so-called RAP-relation, which is a usual normalized relation of the relational model complemented by a set of single-bit label domains. Use of such BLVs allows us to simplify the implementation of relational algebra operations, as well as other non-numerical procedures: a significant part of processing is transferred onto the logical vectors instead of operating with real data.

6.3. Labelled Array Method

In 1984, Suvorov suggested an interesting method of logical processing of arrays, in which the label vectors are even more important. This is the Labelled Array Method (LAM) [75].

The basic idea of the method is the following. All elements of each of the k array arguments participating in the given operation are provided with individual labels so that all elements of the i-th array A_i (i=1,...,k) have the same labels. Out of these arrays, together with the labels, we construct a unified array whose dimensionality is the sum of the dimensionalities of the original arrays. The realization of any given operation consists of two stages. The first, basic, stage is ordering of the unified array with labels; more precisely, it is sorting of labels according to the ordering of the elements of the unified array. Then the second stage is carried out: this constitutes a definite sequence (dependent on the given operation) of common logic operations and certain special operations on the resultant (sorted) BLV. The result of such processing is a binary vector in which the ones denote the elements of the original array which jointly form the resultant array.

Some simple examples will clarify the method, but first we introduce the following definition.

Let A be an arbitrary array arranged in ascending order and containing N elements a_i (i=1,...,N). The *separating vector* of the ordered array A is a binary vector of dimensionality N, containing s ones (s ≤ N), whose i-th digit is given by

$$\varphi_i = \begin{cases} 0, & \text{if } a_i = a_{i+1}, \\ 1, & \text{if } a_i \neq a_{i+1}, \end{cases} \quad (i = 1,...,N-1), \quad \varphi_N = 1.$$

Thus, the ordered array A is separated by the vector φ into s subarrays $A^1,...,A^r,...,A^s$ so that all elements in the r-th array A^r are the same. At the same time, the positions of the ones of the vector φ correspond to the positions of the last elements of s subarrays. All of its other positions contain zeros (Fig.6.3).

Example 1. *Identification of the elements of one array which also appear in another.*

Let A_1 and A_2 be unordered arrays of dimensionalities N_1 and N_2, respectively, such that the operation of union can be performed on these arrays. It is necessary to single out the elements of array A_1 entering into array A_2. According to the method, we construct the unified array $A = (A_1, A_2)$ of dimensionality $N = N_1 + N_2$ consisting of the original arrays A_1 and A_2. The unified array A is supplied with the original binary label vector l of dimensionality N, which marks by ones the elements of array A_1, and by zeroes the element of array A_2 (Fig.6.4). We sort the elements of the unified array together with the corresponding labels so that the elements of array A are located in increasing order. As a result, we obtain the ordered unified array A′ and the sorted label vector l′ (Fig.6.4). For an ordered array A′ we can always construct its separating vector φ according to the rule presented above.

A procedure which transforms the original unified array A (together with the corresponding labels) so that the elements of array A are in increasing order is called the *ordering operation* **A** [A,l] A′,l′,φ. Here a unified ordered array A′, an ordered label vector l′, and a separating vector φ are formed.

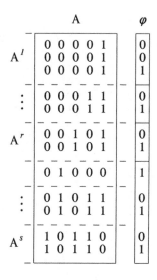

Fig.6.3. Separating vector φ.

Having carried out the operation **A**, we obtain the vector φ, containing s ones, which separates the ordered array A' into s subarrays, and divides the vector 1' into s segments; at the same time, to each r-th subarray there corresponds its r-th segment of the vector 1' (r = 1,...,s) (see Fig.6.4). Note that the ones of the vector 1' correspond to the elements of the array A_1 in A'.

The binary vector of dimensionality N in which ones correspond to the elements of the array A_1 from A' which enter into A_2 is called *entry vector* y. For the operation considered, the vector y is the result. It can be formed from vectors φ and 1' using the following considerations.

If the r-th segment of 1' contains zeros and ones, then the r-th subarray contains elements from A_2 (marked by zeros) and from A_1 (marked by ones). Since all elements of the r-th segment are the same, the elements of array A' corresponding to ones of 1' in the r-th segment are elements of A_1 and enter into A_2. In this case the contents of the r-th segment of the vector y coincides with the contents of the r-th segment of 1' (Fig.6.4). If the r-th segment of 1' contains only zeros (ones), then the r-th subarray contains only

118

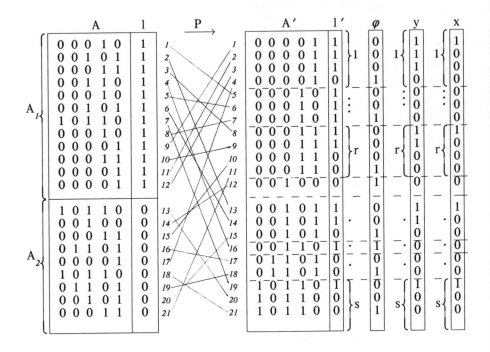

Fig.6.4. Example of LAM operation.

elements from $A_2(A_1)$. In these cases the r-th segment of the vector y must contain only zeros (Fig.6.4). All segments of the vector $1'$ can be analyzed in this way.

A procedure which constructs the vector y from the separating vector φ and the binary vector $1'$ using the rules presented above is called the *special operation* $\Phi(\varphi,1') = y$. The dimensionalities of vectors φ, $1'$, y are the same.

Thus, having carried out, after the operation of ordering $\underline{A}$, the special operation $\Phi(\varphi,1') = y$ on the binary label vectors, we obtain the binary vector y which marks by ones the elements of A' which belong to A_1 and enter into A_2 at the same time. The elements singled out are arranged in increasing order.

Example 2. *Determination of complete entry of one array into another.*

From the rule of forming the entry vector y presented above it follows that if the array A_1 completely enters into array A_2, then among the s segments of l' there are no segments which contain only ones; consequently, in this case any r-th segment (r = 1,...,s) of l' must contain at least one zero.

Thus, if $A = (A_1, A_2)$ and l is the label vector (Fig.6.4), then the sequence of operations **A** $[A,l] \rightarrow A', l', \varphi$; $\Psi(\varphi, l') = r$ forms r = 1 if A_1 enters into A_2; it forms r = 0 otherwise. In the example shown in Fig.6.4 r = 0, since the second and sixth segments contain only ones.

Example 3. *Intersection of two arrays.*

The intersection of arrays A_1 and A_2 is the array $A_3 = A_1 \cap A_2$ consisting of elements of A_1 entering into A_2 and not containing duplicate elements.

The special operation $\Xi(\varphi, z) = x$ is a procedure which constructs from the separating vector φ and some label vector z the vector x according to the rule: if the r-th segment of z contains one or more "ones" then in the r-th segment of x the only "one" is found in the same position as the "one" of the r-th segment of z closest to the (r-1)-st segment; if, however, the r-th segment of z contains only zeros, then the r-th segment of x (r = 1,...,s) is completely zero. The dimensionalities of φ, z, x are the same.

Thus, if $A = (A_1, A_2)$ is a unified array and l is the label vector, then the sequence of operations **A** $[A,l] \rightarrow A', l', \varphi$; $\Phi(\varphi, l') = y$; $\Xi(\varphi, y) = x$ produces the vector x (Fig.6.4) marking by ones the elements from A' forming the array $A_3 = A_1 \cap A_2$.

In the examples given above, in accordance with the LAM method, the ordering operation **A** forms the first stage of processing, while the sequences of common logic operations $(\&, \lor, \neg)$ and special operations (like Φ, Ψ, Ξ) form the second stage.

It can be shown that for a broad range of information problems the logic processing of arrays can be replaced by relatively simple logic processing of label vectors, after application of the operation **A** to the argument arrays.

It is natural to use the LAM method as one of the approaches to support relational databases. In [75] it is shown that with appropriate extension of the set of special operations on label vectors, this methods ensures efficient parallel realization of all the operations of relational algebra.

The labelled array method is essentially a universal method of solving information problems, though many of them (for instance, those which reduce to a limited number of associative searches) do not require preordering, and can be efficiently implemented by simpler means (see Chapter 3).

Now, we consider two other interesting proposals, Positional Sets, and Combinatorial Memory.

6.4. Positional sets

Hardgrave at al. [36] proposed to use the so-called positional sets for representation and manipulation of data in database systems.

The main point of positional sets theory is the recursive definition of a set S called a *positional set*:

$$S := [a_1^{i1}, a_2^{i2}, ..., a_n^{in}],$$

where a_k are called *element identifiers*; they are generalized variables, which may be:

- atoms: integers, reals, literal strings;
- positional sets (different from S);
- names of atoms, or other positional sets.

The symbols i_j are *positional identifiers*, i.e. generalized variables, which may be:

- atoms;
- names of other atoms.

Positional sets can be also defined by:

- enumeration;
- abstraction.

Two approaches are possible. The first consists in enumeration of all duplexes of a positional set. Thus, for instance, the tuple T:

NAME	AGE	SALARY
Jones	30	30000

can be defined by enumeration as follows:

$$T = [\text{ Jones}^{NAME}, 30^{AGE}, 30000^{SALARY}].$$

The second alternative is abstraction. A positional set can be defined by membership conditions, using primitive formulas. The conventional definition of a set by abstraction uses the form:

$$S := \{ z:P \}.$$

This is read as "S is the name of the set of elements z such that P is true", where z is a variable, and P a primitive formula containing z at least once.

Using the positional sets theory, one may define other aggregates: sets, sequences, and tuples. A conventional set may be defined as:

$$\{ a_1, a_2, a_3, \dots , a_n \} - [a_1^{\#}, a_2^{\#}, a_3^{\#}, \dots , a_n^{\#}],$$

where # is the identifier of a special (empty) position.

A sequence may be defined as:

$$< a_1, a_2, a_3, \dots , a_n > = [a_1^{1}, a_2^{2}, a_3^{3}, \dots , a_n^{n}]$$

Positional identifiers are here integers beginning with 1, though for a positional set the order of its elements is irrelevant.

The positional sets theory define also elegantly the tuples of the relational model. Headings of columns are used as positional identifiers. In contrast to sequences, the positional identifiers are not assumed here to be ordered, which enables to exchange the columns of a relation without complications.

If, for example, a personnel relational database contains tuples with positions, then

$$[\; X^{EMP\_NO}, \; Y^{SS\_NO}, \; Z^{EMP\_NAME}, \; U^{SAL\_HIST}, \; V^{EMP\_HIST} \;]$$

is a record of an employee, if every element (for instance, Z) belongs to the definition domain associated with the identifier of the corresponding position.

The use of positional sets enables a quite simple representation of data in memory and their processing.

For practical use the positional identifiers and element identifiers should be encoded by positive integers. This is performed, for instance, by means of *value tables*, which are initiated in the memory for each position (attribute). Each of these tables contains copies of values of the elements of positional sets, and is filled as soon as the element are input into the database. The value of the element need not necessarily be a number; it can be a name, or an identifier of a certain data structure. The essential condition here is that each element should enter the table just once, independently of the context. To each copy of an element entering the table, a corresponding ordering number is assigned. The value table can be used in one of two modes, direct and converse. In direct mode, the value of an element is input, and the output is the ordering number of this value in the table. In indirect mode, the ordering number of the value is input, and the table returns the value of the element.

Further transformation consists in producing of Logical Bit Strings (LBS) corresponding to the incoming positional sets. The main component is here the mechanism of one-to-one mapping of the set of ordered pairs of integers onto the set of integers. One of the possible mappings is the diagonal mapping of Cauchy-Cantor.

Fig.6.5 shows the mapping for the ordered pair (k,l), where k is the number of the row, and l the number of the column. The integer corresponding to this pair (or the position number of "one" in LBS) is found at the intersection of the k-th row and l-th column.

	1	2	3	4	5	6	7	8	9	← 1
1	1	3	6	10	15	21	28	36	45	
2	2	5	9	14	20	27	35	44		
3	4	8	13	19	26	34	43			
4	7	12	18	25	33	42				
5	11	17	24	32	41					
6	16	23	31	40						
7	22	30	39							
8	29	38								
9	37									

↑
k

Fig.6.5. Diagonal table of Cauchy-Cantor.

The use of Cauchy-Cantor mapping is shown in the following example. Suppose that messages

$$S_1 = [21^1, 36^2, 91,2^3] \quad \text{and} \quad S_2 = [36^1, 21^2, 91,2^3]$$

are to be encoded. Assume that the values of the elements are stored in the value table under the numbers 1,2,3, as shown in Fig.6.6.

No.	Value
1	21
2	36
3	91,2

Fig.6.6. Element value table.

Then the results of transformation are messages S_1' and S_2' differing from S_1 and S_2 in that, instead of the values of the elements, their ordering numbers in the value table are put in corresponding positions, i.e.

$$S_1' = [1^1,\ 2^2,\ 3^3] \quad \text{and} \quad S_2' = [2^1,\ 1^2,\ 3^3],$$

which is equivalent to

$$S_1'' = \{<1,1>,\ <2,2>,\ <3,3>\} \quad \text{and} \quad S_2'' = \{<2,1>,\ <1,2>,\ <3,3>\}.$$

Using the Cauchy-Cantor mapping (Fig.6.6) for each ordered pair of sets S_1'' and S_2'', we get the numbers of positions of LBS, values of which are "1", that is,

$$S_1''' = 1000100000001 \quad \text{and} \quad S_2''' = 0110000000001.$$

6.5. Combinatorial Memory

Another method of numeration is used in the so-called Combinatorial Memory, proposed by Kapustyan et al. [52].

Here, to any object (i.e., element of a set) a single integer is assigned, formed by means of what is called a Combinatorial Attribute Tree (CAT). This is a multilevel tree fixing the semantics of some subject domain. In Fig.6.7, an example of a simple CAT is shown. This tree has four levels. All its nodes are numerated. The root, level i labelled by 1, corresponds to the object itself. Level ii describes the independent attributes a,b,c,d, the attribute a taking five different values, numbered 2,3,4,5,6, and the attribute d taking two values (53,54). Levels iii and iv represent the parent-child relationship and contain, in this case, two combinatorial subtrees, the first, with its root in the node 8, describing attributes e and f, and the second, with its root 42, describing attributes g and h.

Numeration of the nodes, in the presence of subtrees, represents the possibilities provided by these subtrees. Thus, as in the node (root) 8 twenty four (4x6) combinations of the attributes e and f are generated, the following node of level ii has as its number 32 (8+24).

It is evident that, to every acceptable set of attribute values there corresponds a unique set of node numbers, or a unique "attribute tree".

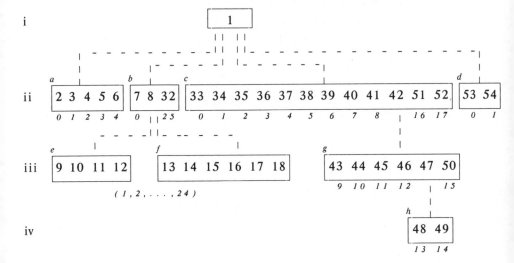

Fig.6.7. Example of combinatorial attribute tree.

Coding of any object from the given domain consists in constructing its attribute tree, and then in computing, for this specific attribute tree, its number. The last computation is performed using a polyadic number system, i.e. a positional system in which the basis of each position is an arbitrary integer, the weight of the least significant position is 1, and the weight of any other position equals the product of the bases of all positions to the right of the former.

Polyadic systems with different sets of bases correspond to different CATs. Fig.6.7 can be associated with a four-digit polyadic system with bases (from left to right) 5,26,18,2. Indeed, the least significant position (d) has only 2 alternatives (or "ciphers"), 53 and 54, to which we assign the conventional symbols 0 and 1; the position (c) has 18 alternatives, to which ciphers 0,1,2,...,17 are assigned; the position (b) has 26 alternatives 0,1,2,...,25, and the position (a) has 6 alternatives 0,1,2,...,5.

In Fig.6.7 the ciphers of positions (a),(c),(d) label each alternative directly.

Somewhat more complicated is the assignment of ciphers in position (b). Ciphers 1,2,...,24 correspond here to various combinations of attributes (e),(f) and may be found, for instance, from the following table:

Table 6.1.

	13 14 15 16 17 18	$\leftarrow f$
9	1 2 3 4 5 6	
10	7 8 9 10 11 12	
11	13 14 15 16 17 18	
12	19 20 21 22 23 24	

$\uparrow$
e

Thus, in the number system just constructed the weights of positions a,b,c,d equal, correspondingly, to 1,2,36,936. The range of numbers (objects) representable in this system, is

$$1 \times 2 \times 36 \times 936 = 67392.$$

Consider an example. Let an object K, from the object domain represented in Fig.6.7, have attributes 5,(10,17),45,54. The polyadic number corresponding to this object has in its least significant position d, the cipher 1 (alternative 54); in position c, the cipher 11 (see Table 6.1); in position b, the cipher 9; and, last, in the most significant position a, the cipher 3.

To obtain the number of this object, it is necessary to compute the decimal number equivalent to the given polyadic. This is done by means of the common rule it is the sum of the products of the position ciphers by corresponding weights:

$$v_K = 3 \times 936 + 9 \times 36 + 11 \times 2 + 1 \times 1 = 3155.$$

Thus, the coding is completed.

However, in this system the numbers of the objects need not be stored. Instead of a number, it is sufficient to store a single bit in the v_K-th position of some Logical Bit String, or a "bit point" (which is, essentially, a UPC). Moreover, a further natural compression of information is possible: for each object only the ordinal number of the corresponding position in LBS z_{bit}, and the distance of this bit from the preceding one, z_{dis}, have to be stored in memory. The database that must store information on N objects reduces thus to a list of N pairs of integers $<z_{bit}, z_{dis}>$.

All information concerning an object is restored by inverse transformation into the polyadic system, with subsequent analysis of the initial combinatorial tree.

The method of coding described above ensures that all the properties of an object are implicitly characterized by the position of its "bit point" on the LBS. Moreover, if the position v_A is assigned to an object A with known properties, and if there exists another "bit point" in some position v_B which is near to v_A on the LBS, then one can state *a priori* that the object B is very similar to the object A. In this sense, any database presented in the combinatorial memory is somewhat similar to the Periodic System of Mendeleev.

In hardware implementation of non-numerical processors by means of the methods described above, a significant part of processing consists in different manipulations with binary vectors (bit strings). Apparently the λ-structure (Chapter 4), the basic operations of which are specifically oriented towards processing binary vectors (compression, counting the number of ones, determination of the position of the k-th "one", a.s.o.) may found here broad applications. The same concerns as well some other DF-structures.

6.6. *Modular Non-Numerical Computer*

In accordance with the specialization principle, one needs different dedicated devices, depending on data structure and processing technology. As an example of such a differentiated approach, consider the modular architecture of the database machine shown in Fig.6.8.

Initial data and results are stored in a memory with vertical access. It is assumed that all functions of the relational DBMS are divided into three classes, depending on the appropriate "processing technology" for implementing different functions.

Class A. Functions based on distributed associative or vertical (quasi-associative) processing. While implementing these functions, the elements of the argument arrays (relations) are analyzed in

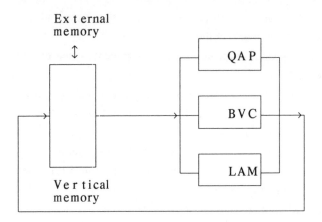

Fig.6.8. Modular DBM.

their original form, without any preprocessing. To this class belong:
- extremal searches (maximum, minimum);
- threshold searches;
- between-the-limits and out-of-the-limits searches;
- component-wise comparison of arrays according to various criteria.

Hardware means appropriate for efficient realization of these functions were described in Chapter 3. In Fig.6.8, QAP (Quasi-Associative Processing) denotes this hardware.

Class B. Functions based on binary vector compression. The main point of this processing technique is that bit-slices of argument arrays (or label vectors) are compressed before proper processing.

We have considered several examples of the application of compression in previous Chapters. With regard to the functions of DBMS, this operation can be used, e.g., for implementing aggregate functions:

total - counting the sum of all elements of an array; can be realized by means of pipeline vertical adder (Chapter 5);

count - counting the number of ones in a binary vector; this is a particular case of "total" operation, when only one bit-slice is input to the vertical adder;

any - a particular case of "count" operation, when the result is not equal to zero: conjunction of all bits of the output register of the vertical adder;

average = total/count, where a concluding division operation is needed.

In Fig.6.8., BVC (Binary Vector Compression) denotes the hardware of class B.

Class C. Whereas for functions of Classes A and B arguments are usually an array and a scalar, Class C contains functions whose arguments are two arrays, or more; and results, in general, are also arrays. To this Class belong such operations of relational algebra as intersection, difference, join, projection. To realize efficiently the functions of Class C, it is expedient to use a hardware subsystem based on the labelled arrays method LAM (see above).

In the Fig.6.8, LAM denotes the hardware of Class C.

6.7. *Set Intersection Processor (ω-structure)*

To conclude this Chapter, consider one more cellular array for massive non-numerical processing, called the Set Intersection Processor (SIP) It is a two-dimensional homogeneous structure of size $m_1 \times m_2$ (Fig.6.9), each cell of which contains an equivalence circuit, a response flip-flop, and some additional logic, which is needed for implementing in this cell sequential bit-wise comparison of corresponding elements of argument arrays M_1 and M_2. After completion of the comparison cycle (of n steps, where n is the length of the element), in the two- dimensional response field of SIP the resulting Binary Label Matrix (BLM) is formed.

Presence of "1" in the (i,j)-th node of BLM means that the i-th element of array M_1 coincides with the j-th element of array M_2.

The SIP is a quasi-associative processor with a higher level of parallelism than conventional associative processors. Whereas in conventional quasi-associative processors all the elements of an

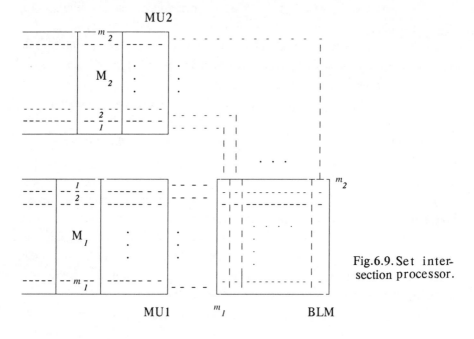

Fig.6.9. Set intersection processor.

argument array coinciding with *one comparand* are singled out during one cycle of memory interrogation, in the SIP a *complete intersection* of two arrays is realized in the same time.

CHAPTER 7

Interconnection Networks

7.1. *Introduction*

In contemporary parallel computing systems, as well as in control and communication systems, the problem of interconnections and data transfer between different units becomes particularly important. This is due to a variety of reasons. First of all, to realize potential high performance and to achieve maximal efficiency of the system, thorough coordination of all units (subsystems) is necessary. In practice, any data processing consists of alternating phases of proper processing (e.g., computations) and exchange of data between subsystems. When the degree of parallelism increases, the arrays which can be processed by separate units become rather large. Thus, it becomes necessary to transfer large data arrays between the processing units in acceptable time and without errors.

Then, for efficient use of some of the parallel algorithms certain formatting or rearranging of input/output data is necessary. For example, in systolic processing the coefficients of incoming matrices should be sent (row-wise or column-wise) to certain PE inputs of the respective systolic array in the form of a polygon of a given shape. Sometimes, sequences of coefficients must be interleaved with zeros.

We see thus that parallel computing systems require not only sufficiently fast data transfer between subsystems, but also efficient auxiliary processing, which might be called Data Structure

Transformation (DST). The procedures of DST include specific operations such as masking, duplication, interleaving, etc.

In processing large arrays in parallel systems, the problems of data transfer and data structure transformation are often more difficult than those of proper computing.

Specialized devices intended for interconnection between different units of a system, or between different users (subscribers, in communication systems), are called *interconnection networks* (ICN) or *commutators*. It should be noted that commutators were first introduced for the needs of telephony, and were probably the earliest example of homogeneous data processing structures. A voluminous literature exists concerning the theory and applications of interconnection networks (see, e.g., [12]). Here we confine ourselves to the main definitions of the theory of interconnection networks, and a short description of most of the common networks and data structure transformation devices. Then we consider the possibilities of using DF-structures as interconnection networks.

7.2. Definitions

An interconnection network is an (N,N)-port device implementing different permutations of N *input data channels*. Besides N input and N *output data channels*, the ICN has a set of *control channels* bringing control signals ensuring setting of the ICN to the given permutations. Transferring of the input array through the ICN is performed sequentially by bit slices (vertically). Therefore, the time of commutation is proportional to the word length of the elements of the array transferred.

The ICNs can be classified according to various characteristics:

1. For connection capabilities:

Connectors, in which any specified previously unused input may be connected to any specified previously unused output.

Concentrators, in which any specified previously unused input may be connected to some arbitrary previously unused output.

Expanders, in which any specified input may be connected to several specified outputs.

2. For control modes:
ICNs with *centralized* control, and
ICNs with *distributed* control (self-control).

3. For ability to establish new connections:
Non-blocking, if the ICN allows addition of arbitrary new interconnection when it has already some arbitrary interconnections.

Rearrangeable, if establishing of a new interconnection in the ICN requires rerouting of one or several interconnections that existed earlier.

Blocking, if there exist interconnection sets that will prevent some new interconnection even with rearrangement of existing interconnections.

4. For internal structure (topology):
Regular and *irregular, one-stage* and *multi-stage, static* and *dynamic* interconnection networks.

In static ICNs the interconnections between inputs and outputs are passive, and do not change during work. In dynamic ICNs, on the contrary, reconfiguration is possible by means of appropriate setting of active switching elements.

Consider here two examples of widely known ICNs.

Fig.7.1 shows the structure of a crossbar switch, which is a regular one-stage dynamic interconnection network with centralized control. This is a non-blocking connector. The crossbar switch in Fig.7.1 has size 4 x 4.

In each of its node an elementary switch is placed, which can be in one of two states: open and closed (see Fig.7.2). To establish a connection between the i-th input and the j-th output of the crossbar switch, it is sufficient to set the (i,j)-th element of the matrix onto the closed state.

134

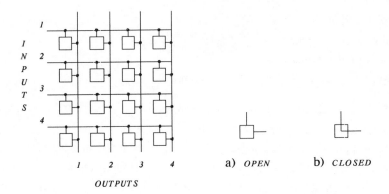

a) *OPEN*   b) *CLOSED*

Fig.7.1. Crossbar switch.   Fig.7.2. Two states
                                    of elementary switch.

Fig.7.3 shows the structure of the so-called Ω-network (for N = 8). This ICN, proposed by Lawrie in 1975 [58], is of fundamental importance for contemporary interconnection systems, and will be discussed in some detail later on. The switching element of an Ω-network (Fig.7.4) can be in one of two states: s = 0, the straight connection (Fig.7.4.a), and s = 1, the exchange (Fig.7.4.b). Such an element is sometimes called *E-cell* (E for Exchange).

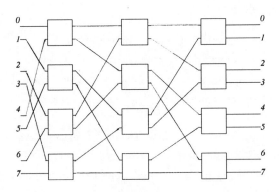

Fig.7.3. Ω-network.

a) straight connection   b) exchange   Fig.7.4. E-cell.

The Ω-network is a regular multi-stage dynamic network. It realizes only some of all possible connections, and can work under centralized control, as well as under distributed control.

5. Another criterion for classifying ICNs is the constructive basis, that is, the type of elementary cells performing the switching in the nodes of the network. We mentioned above two such elements: the crossbar switch and the E-cell. Other switching elements are also used, some of which will be considered later on.

6. One of the possible classification criteria is the bandwidth of interconnections. Each interconnection can be a single-wire link (serial transfer), or a full bus (parallel transfer).

7.3. Functional Possibilities of Interconnection Networks

A connector, or a universal ICN, realizes arbitrary connections, that is, arbitrary one-to-one mappings of N input channels into N output channels, which are represented by arbitrary permutations of the numbers 0,1,...,N-1:

$$P = \begin{bmatrix} 0, & 1, & 2, & ..., & N-1 \\ D_0, & D_1, & D_2, & ..., & D_{N-1} \end{bmatrix},$$

where D_i ($0 \leq i \leq N-1$) is the number of an output channel which has to be connected with the i-th input channel (*destination tag*). The sequence $\{D_0, D_1, D_2, ..., D_{N-1}\}$ is called the *permutation vector*. For large N this notation is, of course, inconvenient. Besides, for many applications, particularly for interconnection between the processors and the memories in parallel systems, it is important to provide for implementation not of the general, but of some special permutations, which usually exhibit some regularities. To describe such permutations, algebraic notations are used, based on various transformations of binary expansions of numbers (indexes) of input channels. Consider this with specific examples.

Let $x_{n-1}, x_{n-2}, ..., x_1, x_0$ be the coefficients of the binary expansion of the index of some input channel of the ICN ($n = \log_2 N$).

A special permutation σ is determined by means of a transformation

$$\sigma\ (x_{n-1}, x_{n-2}, ..., x_1, x_0) = (x_{n-2}, x_{n-3}, ..., x_1, x_0, x_{n-1}),$$

that is, by a cyclic shift of the index one position to the left. Fig.7.5 shows a table of transformations of indexes and the corresponding connection graph of the permutation σ, for N = 8.

000	0	$\longrightarrow$	000	0
001	1	$\longrightarrow$	010	2
010	2	$\longrightarrow$	100	4
011	3	$\longrightarrow$	110	6
100	4	$\longrightarrow$	001	1
101	5	$\longrightarrow$	011	3
110	6	$\longrightarrow$	101	5
111	7	$\longrightarrow$	111	7

Fig.7.5. Perfect shuffle σ.

The binary vector [n-2,n-3,...,1,0,n-1] is called the *characteristic vector* of σ. As can be seen from the Fig.7.5.a, the permutation vector {0,2,4,6,1,3,5,7} corresponds to σ.

The permutation σ, introduced by Pease [64] and studied by Stone [74], is called the *perfect shuffle*, as it interleaves the numbers of the second half of the input channels (4,5,6,7, for N=8) with the numbers of the first half (0,1,2,3) moved apart.

The perfect shuffle σ has very important applications in the algorithms of parallel processing. It is also basic for the study and design of ICNs. We shall discuss later some topics concerning the σ permutation.

Figs.7.6 to 7.8 show the transformations of indexes and

corresponding interconnection graphs for some other widely used special permutations.

Many other regular permutations generated by various index transformations are described in the literature. As can be seen from the figures shown, to each of these permutations corresponds a simple interconnection network, which can be easily realized by means of a straight connection between the inputs and outputs. These patterns are called sometimes "butterflies".

```
000  0  →  000  0        0 O————————O 0
001  1  →  100  4        1 O        O 1
010  2  →  001  1        2 O        O 2
011  3  →  101  5        3 O        O 3
100  4  →  010  2        4 O        O 4
101  5  →  110  6        5 O        O 5
110  6  →  011  3        6 O        O 6
111  7  →  111  7        7 O————————O 7
```

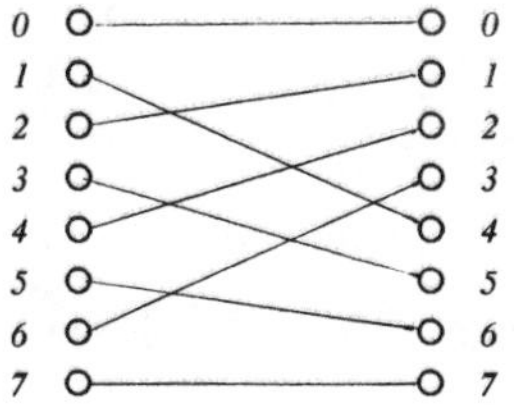

Fig.7.6. Inverse shuffle σ^{-1}: characteristic vector $[0,n-1,n-2,...,2,1]$.

```
000  0  →  000  0        0 O————————O 0
001  1  →  100  4        1 O        O 1
010  2  →  010  2        2 O        O 2
011  3  →  110  6        3 O        O 3
100  4  →  001  1        4 O        O 4
101  5  →  101  5        5 O        O 5
110  6  →  011  3        6 O        O 6
111  7  →  111  7        7 O————————O 7
```

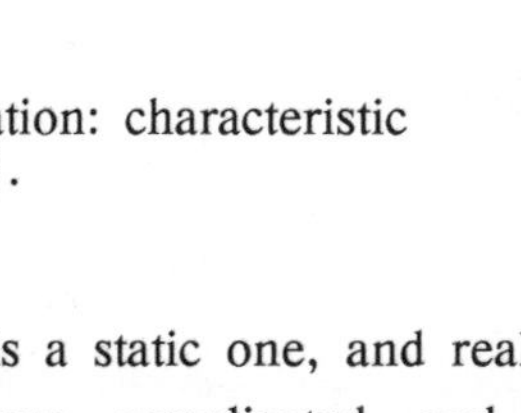

Fig.7.7. Bit reverse permutation: characteristic vector $[0,1,2,...,n-1]$.

Each of these simple, *atomic*, networks is a static one, and realizes only its own permutation. To build more complicated and useful networks, superposition of such atomic networks is used, in combination with dynamic elements. The *exchange* operation, implemented by means of E-cells, is important here.

138

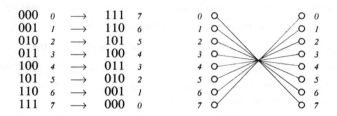

Fig.7.8. Mirror permutation: bit-wise
complementing of indexes.

Consider a homogeneous vertical structure (column) of $N/2$ E-cells (see Fig.7.9.a where $N=8$). Denote $\hat{x} = (x_{n-1}x_{n-2}...x_1\bar{x}_0)$ for all $0 \le x \le N-1$. Then the set of permutations generated by the E-column for different settings of the E-cells is defined as follows.

For any even x $(0 \le x \le N-1)$:

$$e(x)= x \quad \text{and} \quad e(\hat{x})= \hat{x}, \quad \text{for } s=0;$$
$$e(x)= \hat{x} \quad \text{and} \quad e(\hat{x})= x, \quad \text{for } s=1.$$

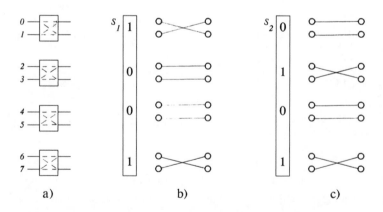

Fig.7.9. E-permutations.

Thus, the set of E-permutations (exchanges) contains $2^{N/2}$ different permutations, corresponding to different settings of the E-cells. Note that, in practice, to set the E-cells on the required states one can use centralized, as well as distributed, control.

Figs.7.9.b and 7.9.c show two examples of E-permutations for N=8 (setting vectors S_1, S_2 and the corresponding butterflies are represented).

Now, using superpositions of static atomic permutations and E-permutations, one can construct flexible and efficient ICNs. To describe this, it is convenient to use structural formulas, which unambiguously characterize the routing of data along the stages of complex (composite) networks. Consider, for example, the so-called *shuffle-exchange network* (Stone's network) [74], very important in various applications, which is a superposition of permutations σ and E, and is described by the structural formula σE.

It is proved that if each of the N channels of the shuffle-exchange network is supplied by a register for storage of intermediate results, and a cyclic processing with corresponding resetting of E-cells in every cycle is organized, then any permutation can be realized by several consecutive runs of the network.

Using the terminology accepted in this book, we can call the shuffle-exchange network a specialized vertical parallel processor.

The Ω-network discussed above (Fig.7.3) is formed by multiple repetition of a shuffle-exchange network, and is described in general by the structural formula

$$\Omega = \sigma E \sigma E ... \sigma E = (\sigma E)^n, \qquad (n = \log N).$$

In practice, distributed multistage networks, based on Stone's network, are widely used. Perhaps the most popular multistage ICN is the Ω-network.

The following important step in development of ICNs was an improvement of an E-cell. The cell was supplemented first by a circuit recognizing combinations of bits at the inputs of the cell: for combinations 00,01,11 the cell is set into the state $s = 0$, and only for combination 10 is it switched into the state s = 1; and secondly by a flip-flop fixing the state of the cell after the setting. The cell thus supplemented is called sometimes a *comparator*.

An Ω-network with comparators in its nodes has a very efficient setting algorithm: it can work as a self-controlling network, in the following manner. If the inputs of the network are fed by binary expansions of destination tags (beginning with the most significant bits), then these bits are the controlling bits for corresponding comparators of consecutive stages.

On the other hand, in an Ω-network *any input* can be connected to *any output*, though after the fixing of such an interconnection many of the other routes become blocked.

The main advantage of an Ω-network is that the subclass of permutations that it realizes (containing only $2^{(N/2)\log_2 N}$ permutations), includes the permutations most important in various applications. Besides, it does not require computation of setting parameters which in other networks takes time of an order $O(N)$, or even $O(N \log_2 N)$. An Ω-network performs a self-control in time of an order $O(\log_2 N)$. The total commutation time consists of the setting time and the time of transferring the input array through the network after setting. The second of these is proportional to the network "depth", i.e. the number of stages. In case of an Ω-network it is proportional to $\log_2 N$. Transferring of the input array is implemented sequentially by bit-slices, which are pulled through the established connections. Such networks are called *flat commutators*, and represent another instance of a vertical operational unit, oriented in this case to interconnection functions.

Among other benefits of the Ω-network note, for instance, that it can be immediately used for the connection of the processors for parallel computation of FFT. Indeed, if one represents the structure of the Ω-network (Fig.7.3) in a slightly changed equivalent form, it becomes evident that it realizes the well known "FFT butterfly".

Various designers tried to construct efficient connectors, that is, networks realizing arbitrary permutations with good time and cost characteristics, on the basis of the shuffle-exchange network. Parker proved in 1975 [63] that any given permutation can be realized at three runs of the Ω-network (which is the same as using a multistage network comprising a superposition of three Ω-networks). The time delay in such a network is proportional to $3\log_2 N$.

Wu and Feng in 1981 [82] improved this result to $(3\log_2 N)-1$. One of the stages of their network was a static permutation δ, that is, it could be replaced by a constant connection between the corresponding nodes. Thus, the whole universal network (connector) is formed of only $(2\log_2 N)-1$ one-stage shuffle-exchange networks. Unfortunately, the Wu-Feng network requires centralized control, the complexity of the control algorithm being $O(N\log_2 N)$.

7.4. Kautz's Interconnection Network

Kautz with collaborators of Stanford Research Institute proposed several variants of interconnection networks [55].

A cell of Kautz's homogeneous interconnection network contains a single-bit register and seven gates. Depending on the state of the register (0 or 1), the cell can perform either of two connecting functions: straight connection (Fig.7.10.a), or switching left-down and up-right (Fig.7.10.b). The basic variant of the network is a triangular matrix built from such cells (Fig.7.10.c). As shown in [55], by appropriate setting of such a matrix an arbitrary permutation of input channels can be obtained.

Indeed, the first column of the matrix consisting of a single cell ensures any permutation of two input channels (Fig.10.a,b); a matrix consisting of two columns ensures any permutation of three input channels (Fig.7.11), etc. In the general case, if a matrix of n-2 columns is already set onto some permutation of n-1 input channels, then, after adding one supplementary, (n-1)-th column and appropriate setting of its cells, one can connect the n-th input channel with any of the n outputs of the enlarged matrix.

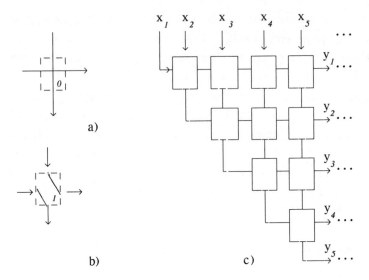

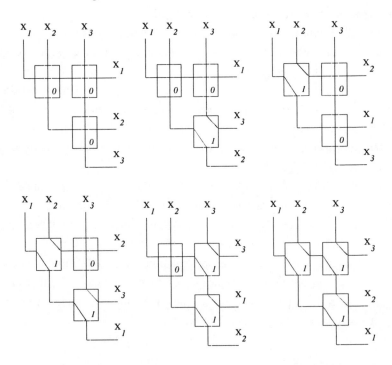

Fig.7.10.Kautz's network.

Fig.7.11. Permutations of 3 input channels.

Fig.7.12 shows, as an example, setting of the (n-1)-th column which provides connection of the n-th input (x_n) with the (n-3)-th output (y_{n-3}).

Cell expenditure for commutation of n inputs is $(n^2-n)/2$. To change for a new permutation, one has to choose a new connection pattern, and perform a corresponding resetting. Setting the memory elements into new states is done sequentially, row by row, which takes considerable time.

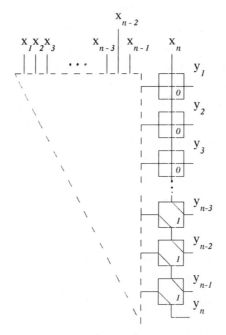

Fig.7.12. Example of setting the network.

There are numerous other ingenious suggestions based on various structures, cells, and control algorithms. We cannot, however, discuss them, because of shortage of space. We now go on to the problems of designing sorting networks.

7.5. Sorting Networks

The importance of the sorting procedure has been already pointed out. Note that this concerns not only data processing in computing systems. Classification and ordering are of special value in many of the natural sciences, such as chemistry, biology, geology, etc.

We call an *ordering* or *sorting* procedure a permutation of the elements of the input (unordered) array which forms an output array where every next element is not less than its preceding element (ascending ordering), or not more than its preceding element (descending ordering).

There is a comprehensive literature on the methods of program sorting in general purpose computers. Knuth devoted one of the volumes of his fundamental work to this problem [57]. Here, we are interested only in parallel hardware implementation of sorting.

In any *universal interconnection* network an ordering can be implemented, as it is a particular case of permutation. Indeed, if for a given input array a rearranging vector $D = \{D_0, D_1, D_2, ..., D_{N-1}\}$ is known, indicating the position of each element of the input array (in which case this vector is called *ordering vector*), then, using any universal ICN and setting the network by means of this vector D, we obtain an ordered array by one run of the network.

If, for instance, the universal network of Wu-Feng is used, then the net time is only $O(\log_2 N)$. However, the calculation of the ordering vector usually has time complexity $O(N \log_2 N)$, and the same time is needed for centralized setting of this network.

Better estimates may be obtained in *self-controlling sorting networks*. Batcher proposed in 1968 [6] two remarkable sorting networks. In these networks the best estimates known are achieved: the ordering of an array of N elements takes $(\log_2 N)^2/2$ steps. We will consider one of Batcher's networks.

7.5.1. *Batcher's Sorting Network*

This network consists of identical hardware units, comparators (Fig.7.13). Two numbers, A and B, are fed to the inputs of the comparator; the lesser of these is obtained on the output L, the greater on the output H. The comparator might be said, thus, to merge chains of length 1 into ordered chains of length 2.

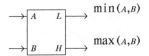
min(A,B)

max(A,B)   Fig.7.13. Batcher's comparator.

Then Batcher gives an iterative rule for the construction of hardware units merging chains of arbitrary length. This rule is as follows.

Suppose the merging block is already constructed for chains of length 2^k. Then the merging unit for chains of length 2^{k+1} can be built from two units for length 2^k, and from 2^{k-1} additional comparators, as described below (see Fig.7.14).

The odd elements of both merged chains are fed in the order $a_1, a_3, a_5, ..., b_1, b_3, b_5, ...,$ to the inputs of the first ("odd") subunit.

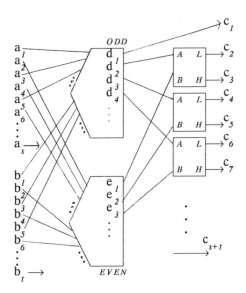

Fig.7.14. Construction of the merging unit.

The even elements $a_2, a_4, a_6, ..., b_2, b_4, b_6, ...$ are fed to the inputs of the second ("even") subunit. At the minimal output of the odd subunit the minimal element of the resulting chain is obtained. At the maximal output of the even subunit the maximal element of the resulting chain is obtained. For all other elements obtained at the outputs of the subunits, an additional comparison is needed, which is implemented by means of additional comparators, so that the i-th comparator compares the i-th output of the even subunit with the (i+1)-th output of the odd subunit, and outputs the 2i-th and (2i+1)-th elements of resulting chain[*].

As an illustration of this rule, Fig.7.15 shows the merging units for chains of length 2 and 4.

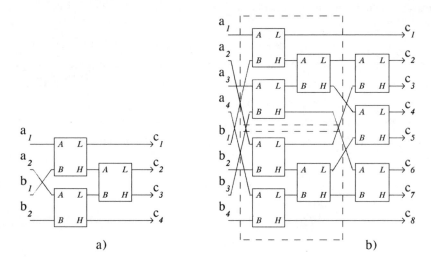

Fig.7.15. Merging units for N=2 (a) and N=4 (b).

The sorting network for an array of size $N=2^p$ is built from merging units as shown in Fig.7.16. At the first stage, chains of length 2 are formed; at the second stage, chains of length 4, etc.

The sorting time required is readily calculated. The longest route passes through $p(p+1)/2$ comparators. Assuming the working time of a single comparator as an elementary step, the whole sorting procedure is seen to take $p(p+1)/2$ steps. In other words, the ordering of an array of N elements takes $(\log_2 N)^2/2$ steps.

---

[*] This iterative rule is justified by the proof given in an Appendix to Batcher's paper [6].

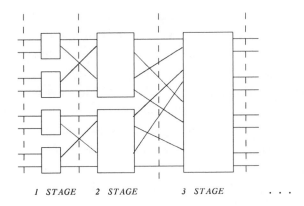

I STAGE   2 STAGE   3 STAGE   . . .

Fig.7.16. General construction of Batcher's network.

7.6. Sorting in DF-structures

Note first of all that when a DF-structure operates as a content-addressed memory (α, ε, and others), any of the algorithms of ordered retrieval is applicable.

In particular, in the 2α-structure, the most efficient of these, Levin's algorithm [60] can be used.

To implement this method the matrix must ensure associative search, and allow the states "0","1", and "X" in each column of the 2α-matrix to be distinguished. The first feature is the proper destination of the 2α-matrix. Show that it has also the second. Indeed, the signal $x'_{Nj} = 0$ ($j = 1,3,5,...$) at the output of the disjunctive chain means that all the words of the matrix have zeros in the j-th position (the state "0"). As in the next even column of the matrix, by condition, are written the complemented values of the j-th bit, the signal $x'_{N,j+1} = 0$ means that all words have ones in the j-th position (state "1"). The situation $x'_{Nj} = x'_{N,j+1} = 1$ corresponds to the state "X" in the α-matrix.

Though the Levin method requires 2N-1 steps, in some cases it may be more efficient than the method of consecutive maximum search (which requires N steps), as all the disjunctive chains operate concurrently, and therefore the parameter N enters the estimation of the step duration as a summand, rather than as a factor.

The functional features of an α-structure ensure also efficient ordered retrieval between-the-limits. To achieve this, the boundary values P (the lower limit) and Q (the upper limit) are put into arbitrary, but especially labelled, rows of the α-matrix (which are called, say, rows N1 and N2), and are processed along with all elements of the argument array. The operation consists, as usual, of a series of consecutive steps of *selection* of maximal elements, whereas the *retrieval* of elements to be included in the resulting array is made beginning with selection of row N1, and ending with selection of the row N2.

The method of detection of the boundary values during the data search procedures described above allows efficient implementation of various data processing problems.

A further increase in efficiency of ordering may be achieved in DF-structures realizing the basic operations GTS (Greater-Than Search) and LTS (Less-Than Search).

1.Hardware implementation of the insertion method

The initial unordered array is placed in a separate memory unit. The resulting ordered array is formed in a matrix of memory elements of the DF-structure of size m x n. Before beginning of the operation, all memory elements of the DF-structure should be cleaned.

Consider ascending ordering. In each cycle the next element of the unordered array is fed to the comparand register of the processor, and the microinstruction GTS is performed. The contents of all selected rows (i.e., the elements greater than the given one) are shifted one position down, and the given element is rewritten from the comparand register into the row that has become empty.

Descending ordering using the insertion method may be organized similarly by means of the microinstruction LTS.

2. Hardware implementation of the counting method

As in the first case, in each cycle the next element is fed to the comparand register, and the microinstruction GTS is performed. The signals of all selected rows are fed to the inputs of a "ones" counter of some type. At the outputs of this counter a binary number is produced indicating the ordering number of the given element in the resulting ordered array. This number is rewritten into the memory of position numbers, in the row corresponding to the position of the given element in the initial array. A special field of the DF-structure may be used as a position number memory, or else a separate memory unit (for instance, a content-addressed memory), of size $m \log_2 m$.

3. Hardware implementation of merge sorting

Suppose two independent ordered arrays M1 and M2 are given, each of m elements, which are to be joined into a single ordered array, of size 2m (ascending order is assumed).

Place one of the initial arrays (for instance, M1) into the memory elements of a DF-structure providing the basic operation GTS (memory unit MU1 in Fig.7.17). The second array may be placed in a memory unit of any type (MU2). In addition, a memory unit of capacity 2m for forming the resulting array is needed; this is denoted MU3.

The merging algorithm can be described as follows.

1. Rewrite the next element of the array M2 into the comparand register.

2. Perform in the DF-structure the LTS operation (non-strict equality). If one or more elements of the array M1 are selected, go to step 3; otherwise to 4.

3. Rewrite the selected elements from MU1 into the next positions of MU3, retaining their relative order.

4. Rewrite the element from the comparand register into the next position of MU3.

5. Verify that the array M1 is exhausted. If not, go to 7; otherwise to 6.

6. Rewrite all remaining elements of the array M2 from the memory MU2 into the next positions of MU3, retaining their relative order. Go to 9.

7. Verify that the array M2 is exhausted. If not, go to 1; otherwise, go to 8.

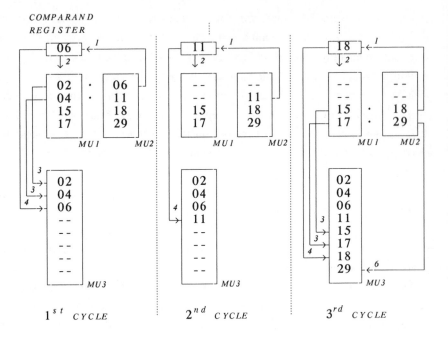

Fig.7.17. Merge sorting in DF-structure.

8. Rewrite all remaining elements of the array M1 from MU1 into the next positions of MU3, retaining their relative order.

9. End of merging.

The operation of this algorithm may be followed on the example shown in Fig.7.17. The numbered lines indicate the data transfers. Numbers at these lines show to what steps of the algorithm corresponds the transfer.

The time of sorting in the scheme just described depends on distribution of values of elements in the argument arrays M1 and M2. In most cases it will be less than for program merge sorting, as at the execution of steps 3,6, and 8 *massive* transfers are used.

7.7. Other Operations of Data Structure Transformation

Up to this point we have considered ICNs performing permutations. It was observed that the permutations most important for organizing interconnections between separate units of parallel computing systems in implementing widely used algorithms belong to special subclasses of all possible permutations.

For these subclasses efficient ICNs were proposed, with short delays and fast setting.

On the other hand, transformations of data structures, which, strictly speaking, are not permutations, have to be performed. We shall describe now the most important of these specific operations, and some specialized devices implementing transformations of data structures.

Several operations of this type has been defined by Feng [21]:

- *Copying*, i.e. duplication of some data elements in two or more copies (elements may be separate bits, words, or bit slices);

- *Masking*, i.e. prohibition of processing of specified array elements;

- *Placing*, i.e. insertion or deletion of blanks in an array, without changing the order of the elements.

Iverson [51] in his language APL proposed a broad range of formal means to describe data transformations. These are the so-called *mixed operations* of APL. Consider some of them.

- *Compression* is an operation, which maps an arbitrary vector f into a vector x, by means of a logical vector z, of size coinciding with the size of f. The result of this operation, vector x, contains only those components f_i of the initial vector f which correspond to $z_i = 1$, while retaining the order of components. The size of vector x is equal to the number of ones in vector z.

- *Expansion* is an operation, which maps an arbitrary vector f into a vector x, by means of a logical vector z, of size not less than the size of vector f. The result of this operation is a vector x, in which the components f_i of the initial vector f occupy positions corresponding to the "ones" of vector z. The size of x coincides with the size of z. The components x_i corresponding to the zeros of z are zeros.

- *Interlacing* is an operation which maps two arbitrary vectors f and g by means of a logical vector z into a vector x whose i-th component coincides with the next component of f if $z_i = 0$, and coincides with the next component of g if $z_i = 1$. The size of x coincides with the size of z and is equal to the sum of the sizes of vectors f and g.

7.7.1. *Flip Network*

Batcher proposed and realized in the STARAN computers an original and very efficient interconnection network called the *Flip network*. This network has N data inputs and N data outputs, as well as $n = \log_2 N$ control inputs to which n-bit control vectors F are fed, setting the network into one of $2^n = N$ possible *Flip permutations* .

Interconnections between input and output nodes are determined by the index transformation :

$$\varphi(x_{n-1}x_{n-2}...x_1x_0) = (x_{n-1} \oplus f_{n-1}, \; x_{n-2} \oplus f_{n-2}, \; ..., \; x_1 \oplus f_1, \; x_0 \oplus f_0),$$

where $(f_{n-1}f_{n-2}...f_1f_0)$ are the coefficients of the binary expansion of the control vector F.

In Fig.7.18 all the eight possible Flip permutations are shown, for n = 3. If the control vector has only one "one", then the corresponding permutation is called *atomic*. For n = 3 there are three atomic permutations A_{001}, A_{010}, A_{100}, as shown in Fig.7.18.

An arbitrary Flip permutation may be obtained as a superposition of atomic ones. This leads to a design of a Flip network by consecutive connection of n switching stages, each of which is set by one bit of the control vector, and realizes the corresponding atomic permutation. Fig.7.19 shows the structure of a three-stage Flip network, which belongs essentially to the multistage ICNs with E-cell switching elements, already discussed above. If we remake this scheme as Fig.7.20 (merely interchanging some nodes of the second and third stages), it becomes evident that: a) all stages can be taken as identical (n/2 E-cells in each); b) between the outputs of the preceding stage and the inputs of the following a static permutation σ^{-1} is performed; c) for control of eqach stage, one bit of the control vector is sufficient: if $f_i = 0$, then all E-cells of the i-th stage are in the "straight" state; if $f_i = 1$, then they all are switched into the "exchange" state.

The real Flip network of a STARAN computer is somewhat more complicated than described above. Besides the Flip permutations, it provides for a set of *shift permutations*; each of these is a shift of the input nodes on 2^m positions (mod 2^p), where $0 \leq m < p < n$. Any shift divides 2^n inputs into groups, each of 2^p, and performs a cyclic shift "down" on 2^m positions in each group.

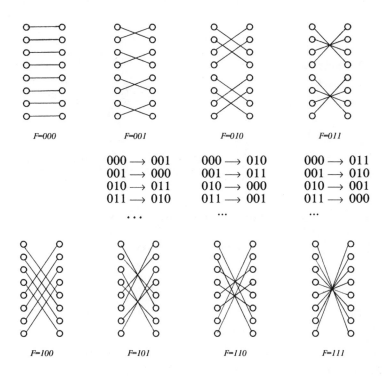

Fig.7.18. Flip permutations.

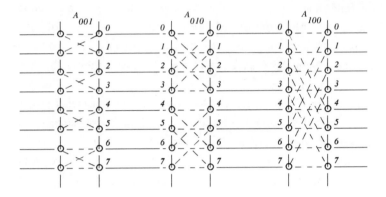

Fig.7.19. Flip network (n=3).

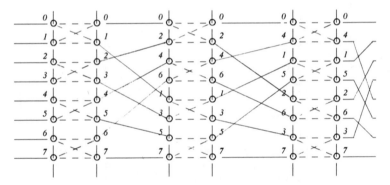

Fig.7.20. Another shape of Flip network.

7.8. DF-structures as Interconnection Networks

7.8.1. α-structure as a Connector

Statement 10. *α-structure is a non-blocking connector with centralized control.*

Consider a square α-matrix of size N x N (Fig.7.21). Let the inputs z of the left boundary be the inputs of the interconnection network we want to build, and the outputs x' of the bottom boundary its outputs.

Suppose it is necessary to connect the i-th input with the j-th output. This can be done by using the α-cells as interconnection elements (see Chapter 4). Clearly, if the (i,1)-st, (i,2)-nd, ... ,

$(i,j-1)$-th cells of the i-th row are set onto the function α_{TR} $(a = 0, \; y = 0)$, then the input z of the (i,j)-th cell becomes connected with the input node of the i-th row. It should be noted that in all the cells set in this way, the channel $x - x'$ is then formed, which can be used in corresponding columns for routing of other connections.

Now, set the (i,j)-th cell onto the function α_{CON}. To do this, it is necessary to feed the constant $x = 0$ to the input x of this cell, which requires, in its turn, to set the $(1,j)$-th, $(2,j)$-th, ...,

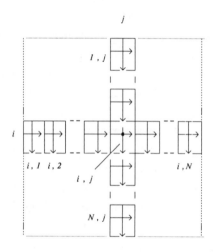

Fig.7.21. Connections in α-structure.

$(i-1,j)$-th cells onto the function α_{TR}, and to feed the boundary constant $x = 0$ to the input x of the $(1,j)$-th cell. A channel $z - z'$ is thus formed in all the mentioned cells of the j-th column, which can be used in the corresponding rows of the matrix for routing of other connections.

Clearly in the (i,j)-th cell the signal from the horizontal channel z of the i-th row is switched into the vertical channel x of the j-th column.

Now, set the $(i+1,j)$-th, $(i+2,j)$-th, ..., (N,j)-th cells of the j-th column onto the function α_{TR}. Then, in these cells a chain x connecting the output x' of the (i,j)-th cell with the output x' of the (N,j)-th cell is formed, concluding the routing of the required interconnection.

As all the cells of the j-th column, except the (i,j)-th, should be set onto the function α_{TR}, the value y = 0 has to be fixed. Hence, in the (i,j)-th cell the same value y = 0 is obtained. This does not prevent, however, the setting of this cell onto the function α_{CON} (by means of inputting a = 0), because the function α_{CON} does not depend on y.

The states of the (i,j+1)-th, (i,j+2)-th, ..., (i,N)-th cells are irrelevant for the interconnections just established. However, to ensure the possibility of independent routing of other interconnections, these cells have to be set onto the function α_{TR}.

Thus, we can formulate the general rule: to connect the i-th input of the α-matrix with the j-th output, it is necessary and sufficient to set the (i,j)-th cell onto the function α_{CON}, and all other cells of the i-th row and the j-th column onto the function α_{TR}.

Suppose that, after connecting the i-th input with the j-th output, we have to connect some k-th input (k ≠ i) with some l-th output (l ≠ j). Following the rule just established, set the (k,l)-th cell onto the function α_{CON} and all other cells of the k-th row and the l-th column onto the function α_{TR}. Clearly, for all relations between k and i, as well as between l and j, such setting is not prevented by the previous setting of cells of the i-th row and j-th column, as in accordance with the same rule, any cell of the i-th row and the j-th column, which must carry the new interconnection, are set onto the function α_{TR}.

Hence, applying the rule N times, one can realize in the α-matrix interconnections between N arbitrary different pairs of input and output nodes. This proves that an α-structure is a non-blocking connector with centralized control.

7.8.2. λ-structure as a Specialized Network

Introduce into a λ-structure (Fig.3.16) a second horizontal channel (a bus) f, in each of its rows, and a second vertical channel g, realizing the function $g' = g \lor \overline{z}\overline{t}f$, in each column. Then the system of logical functions implemented by each cell takes the form:

$$z' = zt, \qquad (7.1)$$
$$t' = z \lor t, \qquad (7.2)$$
$$g' = g \lor \overline{z}\overline{t}f, \qquad (7.3)$$
$$f' = f. \qquad (7.4)$$

Call the resulting scheme a λ_I-structure. We shall prove that the λ_I-structure performs various special functions of an interconnection network.

Definition. A permutation is *compressing* if it connects any ordered M-tuple of specified input channels, from the total number N, with M adjacent output channels, retaining the relative order.

A compressing permutation is determined by a binary control vector Z, in which the necessary input channels are indicated by ones. For instance, if for N = 16 the 3rd, 7th, 8th and 12th input channels should be connected, correspondingly, with the 1st, 2nd, 3rd and 4th output channels, then Z = 0010001100010000.

Statement 11.   *λ_I-structure is a self-setting interconnection network realizing the class of all compressing permutations.*

Let the boundary inputs f_{iI} of the left boundary be the inputs of the interconnection network, and the boundary outputs g'_{Nj} its outputs. The control vector Z is fed bit-wise to the boundary inputs z_{iI} of the left boundary. To the inputs t and g of all cells of the upper boundary the constants $t_{Ij} = 0$ and $g_{Ij} = 0$ are fed.

In each cell where the condition $\overline{z}\overline{t} = 1$ is fulfilled, in accordance with (7.3), $g' = f$; that is, the interconnection function "fork-down" is realized. If in the control vector Z the ones occupy the i_I-th, i_2-th, ..., i_M-th positions, then, as follows from (7.1)-(7.2), the condition $\overline{z}\overline{t} = 1$ appears in the i_I-th row of the 1st column, the i_2-th row of the 2nd column, ..., the i_M-th row of the M-th column. Thus, the outputs g_{Nj} of the 1st, 2nd, ..., M-th columns will be connected with the inputs f_{il} of the i_1-th, i_2-th, ..., i_M-th rows, correspondingly.

Hence, the λ_I-structure realizes the necessary interconnections.

The setting of the λ_I-structure onto the given permutation is performed automatically after the control vector is applied to the inputs z, and necessary constants are fed to other boundary inputs. The setting time depends only on the duration of transition processes in the combinational circuits of the structure.

Definition. A permutation is *expanding* if it connects M adjacent input channels with an arbitrary specified M-tuple of output channels, from the total number N, retaining the relative order. An expanding permutation is determined by a binary vector T, in which the necessary output channels are indicated by zeros.

Statement 12. *λ_I-structure is a self-setting interconnection network realizing the class of all expanding permutations.*

As above, the inputs f_{il} of the left boundary are used as the inputs of the network, and the outputs g'_{Nj} as its outputs. The control vector T is fed to the boundary inputs t_{lj} of the upper boundary. To the inputs g of all cells of the upper boundary the constants $g_{lj} = 0$ are fed, and to the inputs z of all cells of the left boundary the constants $z_{il} = 1$.

The principle of operation remains the same as above, but in those columns of the λ_I-matrix where the control vector contains ones, $t_{lj} = 1$. Clearly in such columns the condition $z\bar{t} = 1$ cannot appear, and at the corresponding outputs g'_{Nj} zeros are retained. Other columns perform the required interconnection as follows. Let zeros occupy i_1-th, i_2-th, ..., i_M-th positions in the control vector. Then, as in all rows $z_{il} = 1$, the condition $z\bar{t} = 1$ appears in the 1st cell of the i_1-th column, 2nd cell of the i_2-th column, ..., M-th cell of the i_M-th column. Hence, the 1st, 2nd, ..., M-th input channels will be connected with the i_1-th, i_2-th, ..., i_M-th output channels, which corresponds to the given expanding permutation.

CHAPTER 8

Implementation of Cellular Microprocessors

We have described several specialized homogeneous microprocessors (DF-structures) that implement their basic functions by means of immediate simulation of algorithms in corresponding logic networks.

As was shown, the set of these functions is practically universal, and thus arbitrary schemes for computing devices can be designed on the basis of these structures.

In this Chapter we demonstrate, with examples, the efficient use of the inherent features of DF-structures (such as microparallelism, multifunctionality, quasi-analogue style of processing) in the hardware support of computing systems.

8.1. Specialization

One of the best ways to improve efficiency is by *specialization* of hardware. The source of efficiency is the fact that most computational problems are not of universal character. Separate problems and fragments of algorithms always have specific features which can and must be used.

Even those computers which we now call "general purpose computers" can also be considered as specialized: they are specialized for solving numerical problems by *sequential* performance of arithmetical operations. The data unit processed by such computers in each instruction is a *word* (number). This classical (von Neumann) architecture was historically connected with those problems for which the first computers were intended (ENIAC, for instance, was intended for calculation of ballistic tables). Such architecture corresponded to universal mathematical theory (arithmetic, mathematical analysis, etc.), which had been developed over centuries.

When the problem of improving computer performance become a vital need, specialists began to seek ways of parallelizing. Particular problems, or classes of problem, were analyzed, in order to discover features of specific data and algorithm structures and to map them into the new parallel architectures; or, which was even more efficient, to design architectures best fitted to various problems.

This is what is meant by specialization.

The principle of specialization is generally accepted in all fields of human activity. In industry, two different kinds of specialization are possible: *product specialization* oriented towards a manufactured object or group of objects; and *technological specialization*, oriented towards types of processes (for example, casting) and thus concerned with the treatment of an object or group of objects.

For the development of computer architecture, specialization of the technological kind seems to be more applicable, intended for efficient realization of the complicated and massive procedures that are often encountered in computational processes, and hence useful in solving large problems of many different classes.

Large and complicated problems have, as a rule, structural organization of data and of operations. Hence, in the processors of the new architectures, structural units are not numbers, as they were in von Neumann computers, but *large blocks*, such as vectors, matrices, tables, graphs, etc. Analysis of typical processing structures and operations allows us to justify the proper selection of structure of the operational units, specific for realization of defined basic procedures.

Sometimes misgivings are expressed that the application area of specialized devices is too narrow. Whether this is so depends on the particular approach to specialization. Analysis of the problems, of basic large-block constructions and processing types, can enable the efficient solution of a broad range of problems with a moderate number of specialized hardware modules (specialized processors) in the system. For applications of particular importance, however, and taking into account the low cost of contemporary integrated circuits, one may consider the hardware expenditure and the loading factor as relatively insignificant, and to be subordinated to the main goal of achieving maximal performance in solving the specific problem.

A good example of technological specialization is associative processing.

The associative processors, initially specialized for the specific tasks of information retrieval, have led gradually to the development of vertical processing systems, considered in Chapter 2. These systems, like vector pipeline systems, have a rather broad application field, and are the second fundamental way forward in supercomputer development.

Homogeneous specialized processors (DF-structures), which are the main theme of this book, may be used in different versions. It is reasonable to distinguish three types of use:

a) as autonomous specialized computing and control instruments;
b) as functional modules as part of general purpose or specialized data processing systems;
c) as coprocessors working in cooperation with some general purpose computer, in heterogeneous environment.

8.2. Autonomous Instruments

Specialized processors are widely used as autonomous devices in special purpose airborne and ground systems, in control systems for certain technological processes, and in robot control systems. Here the main requirements are often diminished size and weight of processors, as well as speed of decision-making.

In these cases, specialized homogeneous processors have to be used in the mode of implementing their basic operations.

8.2.1. *Robot Movement Control*

As an example we shall consider the use of a processor with the basic operation "maximum search" for recognition of critical situations in the object under control. Suppose the memory elements of the rows of an α-processor are continuously fed with values of some parameter from the set of objects under control. The resulting signals at the right boundary of the α-matrix will always indicate that object in which the controlled parameter is maximal.

For the implementation of walking robots, to avoid collisions with obstacles, the coordinates of the robot's legs have to be continuously compared with the coordinates of the obstacles in planning the trajectory of the robot's movement. This problem can be solved by means of an ε-processor as follows.

Assume that for each leg the differences between its coordinates and the coordinates of all obstacles are continuously calculated (note that this calculation is a component-wise operation upon a vector and a scalar). The differences obtained are fed into the rows of the ε-processor, and in the corresponding comparand register the minimal allowable difference is written. Clearly, the operation LTS (Less-Than Search) will dynamically indicate the row corresponding to a dangerous situation, that is, unacceptable proximity of a leg to an obstacle, and will specify the obstacle. Massive parallel processing ensures real-time control of the robot movement trajectories for a large number of legs and/or obstacles.

A similar approach may be used in the real-time control of arbitrary objects, working in complicated or unpredictable situations.

8.2.2. *Measurement and Sorting in Mass Production*

Another example of an autonomous specialized homogeneous processor is the ρ-matrix solving the problem of classifying mass production objects. If in the rows of the ρ-matrix boundary values of given tolerances are written, and values of the measured parameters of objects are fed to the inputs of the ρ-processor, then the signals produced at its right boundary may be used to control the mechanism of the sorting device.

8.3. Functional Modules

8.3.1. *Constructive Blocks of Computers*

In this case, each functional module performs a fixed procedure, thus implementing hardware realization of some subroutine. If a look-up is organized in a general program, and the data are directed for processing into appropriate functional modules, then the central processor of the system is relieved from the execution of corresponding subroutines, in particular, from the inefficient execution of loops in the implementation of massive computations. In such a way, hardware support of the software is realized.

A natural question arises: how many different functional modules have to be used in the system ?

There exists a conflict between the endeavour to implement each massive operation on a special functional module dedicated to it, and the necessity for reasonable limitation of module nomenclature. This conflict can be resolved as follows.

It is known that a DF-structure is most efficient in that operation for which it was hardware-intended. Each DF-structure realizes, as a rule, not only a single, but several, basic operations. In the present case it is not the concrete contents of a given operation that are essential, but only the style of computation involved, that is, the processing type. Several different operations may be similar in the processing type they use, and thus, in their corresponding requirements to the hardware of the functional module. For instance, several elementary functions ($\sin x$, $\operatorname{tg} x$, a^x, etc.) can be realized by some functional module dedicated for computation of polynomials with different coefficients.

It is essential that the total number of functional modules sufficient for real improvement of the efficiency of massive data processing is not too large. Such modules could serve as *building blocks* in the construction of different devices and systems.

In this connection, the idea of the standard processor suggested by Haendler [31] should be mentioned. The idea is that the same processor can work in different modes, depending on the class of problem to be solved. Possible modes are the following:

1. General-purpose processor,
2. High-level-language processor,
3. Reduction machine,
4. Data-flow processor,
5. Associative parallel processor,
6. Cellular processor,
7. Digital differential analyzer.

Haendler supposes that such a multifunctional processor could be switched from mode to mode, being not necessarily seven times more complicated and expensive than each of the listed processors, but, say, twice, because different modes are compatible; or else, the processors may efficiently simulate one another.

A similar situation, but on a lower structural level (the level of functional modules), is found in implementing DF-structures. Indeed, the different DF-structures considered in this book exhibit significant flexibility, multifunctionality and interchangeability. These features are seen, in particular, from the Statements of previous Chapters. For instance, one single functional module α is sufficient to realize *memory* (Statement 1), *arbitrary logical functions* (Statement 3), *arbitrary interconnections* (Statement 10), etc. The application of several types of functional module (e.g., $\alpha, \varepsilon, \lambda$) can give more flexibility (or lower cost) in assembling complicated computing devices. One might say that a set of *specialized* functional modules, which are all the DF-structures described, possesses *universal* properties.

8.3.2. *DF-structures in a Grid Massively Parallel Processor*

The Grid Massively Parallel Processor (GMPP) described in [50] is intended for numerical simulation of large dynamic systems solving computationally intensive modelling processes in geophysics, hydrodynamics, electronics etc. by means of grid methods.

The GMPP is a multiprocessor computing complex of pyramid architecture. At the first level of the pyramid an array of processing elements (PEs) is located. Each PE of this array corresponds to an appropriate node of the grid and computes values of the grid function at this node.

At the second level the devices of shared destination are located, namely, specialized functional processors, buffer memory units, and microprogrammed controllers. Each of these devices is used by the set of nearest PEs of the first level array.

The third level is the main control unit, which organizes the operation of the whole system.

The GMPP is connected with one or several host computers (PCs, workstations, etc.) intended for user and external memory interfaces.

The special feature of the GMPP, distinguishing it from other similar projects, is the use of DF-structures as basic building blocks.

The organization of the interconnection network of the GMPP may serve as an example.

It is known that one of the principal requirements for a computing system intended for implementation of grid methods is the ability to reconfigure the PE array to different stencils, depending on the types of problem to be solved and the algorithms used.

In the GMPP a specialized interconnection network allowing flexible programmable reconfiguration of stencils is used. The network is organized as follows.

Each PE has its own Local Interconnection Module (LIM), Fig.8.1, consisting of a Compressing λ-Network (λCN) of size $p \times q$, and a control block. The p input nodes of the λ-network are connected, by means of single-bit-width buses, with the outputs of p neighbouring PEs corresponding to the necessary set of the standard stencils. The q output nodes of the λ-network are connected with the inputs of q general purpose registers of the considered PE. For a wide range of problems and algorithms, the characteristic values are $p = 16$ or 32, $q = 4$ or 8.

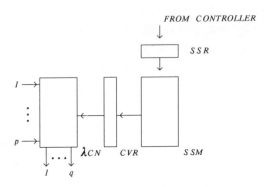

Fig.8.1. Local interconnection module of each GMPP node.

The control block of the LIM contains a Standard Stencils Register (SSR), a Standard Stencils Memory (SSM), and a Control Vector Register (CVR). In the SSM the p-bit control vectors of all necessary stencils are stored. Each of them has a definite number of ones, defining the pattern of the stencil. For rapid changing of stencils over the whole system, it is sufficient to write the code of the new stencil from the system controller (or from the host) into the SSRs of all LIMs. Then, immediately, each LIM produces at the outputs of its SSM the corresponding control vector, and the λ-network connects the inputs of the considered PE with the outputs of those neighbouring PEs which correspond to the new grid stencil.

The modular interconnection network of the GMPP allows also fast resetting of various areas of the PE array to different stencils.

Another example of using DF-structures in the GMPP is for parallel computation of some special functions, the values of which are needed, for instance, in each node and for each iteration in solving non-linear problems.

These functional computations are performed by means of the table interpolation method in specialized Table look-up Functional Modules (TFMs). Since a TFM is a rather complicated hardware device (compared with the PE), the use of a separate TFM in each node is not acceptable. Therefore, in the GMPP parallel multiport TFMs are used, located at the second level of the pyramid. Each of them cooperates with a cluster of nearest PEs of the first level.

In the GMPP the structure of the TFM is similar to that of the table look-up processor (Fig.5.5). However, in this case, several parallel comparators work concurrently, so that the interrogation of the argument table is made *simultaneously* for all arguments x_i coming from the PEs of the cluster served.

8.3.3. *Economical Connector Based on λ-structure*

Interconnection networks based on the λ-structures considered above retain, when performing permutations, the relative order of the elements of argument arrays. To implement arbitrary permutations between N inputs and N outputs, it is necessary, as is well known, to use an ICN with the functional possibilities of a connector. Such networks, for large N, usually have considerable complexity of the hardware and of the setting algorithms.

At the same time, in practice, situations often occur when, at each current time interval, arbitrary connections are needed of no more than M input channels with the same number of output channels (from the total N, where M << N). In such cases, the commutation problem can be efficiently solved by means of a λ-structure, using the following construction.

Consider a scheme from three units, shown in Fig.8.2. Unit 1 is a compressing λ-network, unit 2 is a connector, unit 3 is an expanding λ-network.

Suppose it is necessary to connect M input channels, with arbitrary numbers $i_1, i_2, ..., i_M$ ($i_1 < i_2 < ... < i_M$) with M output channels with arbitrary numbers $j_1, j_2, ..., j_M$. Order the vector $J = j_1, j_2, ..., j_M$ ascendingly. The ordering vector $K = k_1, k_2, ..., k_M$ thus constructed is used as a permutation vector for setting the connector (unit 2). For setting the compressing network, the control vector Z is used, having ones at the i_1-th, i_2-th, ..., i_M-th positions, whereas another control vector T, having zeros at the j_1-th, j_2-th, ..., j_M-th positions, is used for setting the expanding network.

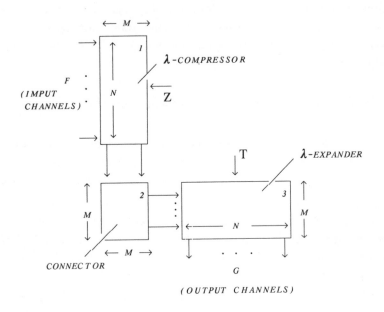

Fig.8.2. Three-stage connector.

We now show that, with the setting just described, this scheme realizes the given arbitrary permutation of M inputs.

According to Statement 11 (Chapter 7), in unit 1 the i_1-th, i_2-th, ..., i_M-th input channels will be connected with the 1st, 2nd, ..., M-th output channels. This order is retained at the inputs of unit 2. In unit 2, according to its setting, the permutation is performed connecting the 1st, 2nd, ..., M-th inputs, respectively, with the k_1-th, k_2-th, ..., k_M-th outputs. As $K = k_1, k_2, ..., k_M$ is, by definition, the ordering vector, the relative order of the permuted elements at the output of unit 2 corresponds to the given relative order in which they should be output at the outputs of the whole scheme. This order is retained also at the inputs of unit 3, which completes the permutation, connecting, according to Statement 12 (Ch.7), its 1st, 2nd, ..., M-th inputs with its j_1-th, j_2-th, ..., j_M-th outputs.

The hardware expenditure in units 1 and 3 of this scheme is NM λ-cells in each. An α-structure (unit 2) working in the interconnection mode (see Statement 10, Chapter 7) may be used as a connector. Then the hardware expenditure in the unit 2 is M^2 α-cells.

8.3.4. *Functional Computations in λ-structure*

These computations are based on a rather unusual property of the λ-matrix.

Consider a λ-matrix of size m x n arranged as in Fig.8.3. If some binary vector F is fed to the inputs z, then, in accordance with the basic algorithm of operation of the λ-matrix (see Chapter 3), each *next* "*one*" of this vector marks by a unique logic condition ($z\bar{t} = 1$) the single cell of the *next row* of the λ-matrix corresponding to its coordinate.

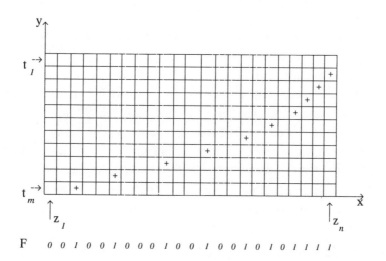

F   0 0 1 0 0 1 0 0 0 1 0 0 1 0 0 1 0 1 0 1 1 1 1

Fig.8.3. Functional mapping in λ-structure.

Suppose an n-bit binary vector F represents the "increment flow" of some continuous function $f(x)$, that is, corresponds to the code of the step function approximating the given function. Clearly, in this case the marked cells are tracing, as it were, a representation of the function's graph on the coordinate grid formed by the cells of the λ-matrix (see Fig. 8.3).

The feature described above allows us to realize, on the basis of a λ-structure, various non-conventional, quasi-analogue devices for computation of functions, A/D and D/A conversions, integration, solving of some equations, etc. The efficiency of these computations is determined by the fact that they are performed by the propagation of signals through the combinational circuit of the λ-matrix, and the results are obtained immediately after the termination of the transition processes.

8.4. Combined Architectures

8.4.1. *The Basis of Combined Architecture*

As already mentioned above, an important reserve of increasing performance of existing computer systems seems to be the broad application of different *problem-oriented processors.*

The use of specialized processors for improving the performance of computing systems is not new. Thus, as early as the 60s, "accelerators" for vector computations appeared on the market: the so-called array processors, already mentioned. Arithmetic coprocessors such as Intel 80387, Motorola MC 68881, Weitek, etc. became widely used; these were intended for speeding up floating point computations.

Coprocessors are distinguished not only by their purpose, but also, of course, by their internal structure. We shall distinguish between specialized processors of homogeneous and of inhomogeneous structure.

Processors of homogeneous structure are of a special interest to us. To this class belong not only the DF-structures but also different cellular automata (see Chapter 3), systolic/wavefront arrays, etc. In many cases, the specialized homogeneous processors achieve record speed of processing in appropriate fields.

However, smooth operation of such processors necessarily requires concerted input and output of data in specified formats, and in proper times. For example, in systolic processing the coefficients of incoming matrices should be sent (rowwise or columnwise) to certain PE inputs of a respective array in the form of a polygon of a given shape. Sometimes, the sequences of coefficients must be interleaved by zeros. If the conventional memory devices and input/output hardware are used, the realization of these elaborate data manipulations leads to serious difficulties, and inevitably reduces the expected performance of the specialized processor.

At the same time, many of the existing parallel systems have powerful means of implementing the input/output and preprocessing of large data arrays. The VPSs (see Chapter 2) are of special interest in this context.

The success of these supercomputers apparently surpassed the expectations of their designers. This architecture, which arose out of an idea of *non-numerical* associative processing, proved to be quite efficient also for solving important large-scale problems of a *numerical* nature. At the same time, one can observe that there is some lack of balance between separate subsystems of the VPS. In VPS, the operational unit is evidently behind other subsystems. Typically, VPS possesses a main memory of very large capacity, a huge mass memory array supported by a high-bandwidth I/O control subsystem, efficient interconnection networks. As to the operational unit, it consists of the simplest single-bit ALUs (though with a high degree of parallelism).

The bit-sequential processing technique used in each PE affects especially the implementation of floating point arithmetic. Moreover, the realization of all basic operations in each PE is done in a standard, universal way, by means of sequential microprograms applied at each step to the next digit of data stored in local memory.

So, the VPSs *do need* accelerators. Homogeneous specialized processors *proved to be* perfect accelerators. Thus, these processors and the VPSs make good pairs.

The above considerations lead to the notion of combined architecture. We call *Combined Architecture* a multiprocessing computing complex in which the solution of each problem is considered as an interaction of several processes, so that execution of each process is delegated to the specialized subsystem most efficient in implementation of this process. The subsystems are controlled in such a way that their balanced operation can be ensured, and special complementing features of subsystems can be best exploited. For each subsystem a structure is chosen which best corresponds to the function it is to perform.

8.4.2. *An Example: the Mixed Associative-Systolic Computer*

One example of a combined architecture is the Mixed Associative-Systolic Computer (MASC) described in [25,80]. This system represents a combination of a STARAN-like VPS with a set of systolic/wavefront processing arrays. It is intended in the first place for solving computation-intensive matrix problems.

As an illustration of the functioning of this system consider the preparation of input data for solving the algebraic path problem for which a set of systolic arrays has been developed by means of a systematic method [69].

Suppose that the initial matrix of the order n with k-bit coefficients is stored rowwise in local memories of n PEs of the basic SIMD system (see Fig.8.4, where $n = 4$).

a_{11}	a_{12}	a_{13}	a_{14}	1ST chan.
a_{21}	a_{22}	a_{23}	a_{24}	2ND chan.
a_{31}	a_{32}	a_{33}	a_{34}	3RD chan.
a_{41}	a_{42}	a_{43}	a_{44}	4TH chan.

$\rightarrow| \; k \; |\leftarrow$

Fig.8.4. Initial placing

o	o	o	a_{14}	a_{13}	a_{12}	a_{11}	$\rightarrow$
o	o	a_{24}	a_{23}	a_{22}	a_{21}	o	$\rightarrow$
o	a_{34}	a_{33}	a_{32}	a_{31}	o	o	$\rightarrow$
a_{44}	a_{43}	a_{42}	a_{41}	o	o	o	$\rightarrow$

$t_7 \quad t_6 \quad t_5 \quad t_4 \quad t_3 \quad t_2 \quad t_1$

Fig.8.5. Necessary shape.

One of the systolic algorithms for solving the problem requires the incoming data in the form shown in Fig.8.5. The corresponding preprocessing is made in the memory of the SIMD-system by means of regular row shifts of the initial matrix: the i-th row ($i = \overline{1,n}$) is shifted in the i-th PE by $k(i-1)$ bits to the right relative to its primary position. The implementation of this procedure in the SIMD system requires only n read-write cycles or $2n$ time steps. The result of preprocessing is shown in Fig.8.6. As can be seen from this figure, the necessary volume of memory is $nk(2n-1)$ bits.

Fig.8.6. Regular row shift.   Fig.8.7. Mask table.

After the described preprocessing we can proceed with reading the data from the memory and transmitting them to the processing (systolic) subsystem. The reading is accomplished by means of standard SIMD-system instructions using necessary masking. The set of masks for the present example is given in Fig.8.7. The time of transmitting is negligible because the data readout and the processing in the systolic array make up a single pipeline.

8.4.3. Heterogeneous Computing

The vast majority of modern supercomputers are based on one of the classical architectures: MIMD, SIMD, vector. It is known that even the most powerful of them allow us to achieve a high *real* performance only for those classes of algorithms and problems which fit adequately into their architecture.

However, the application problems are usually non-uniform. Different problems and various fragments of the same problem can successfully exploit the high performance characteristic of different architectures (SIMD, MIMD, vector, special, etc.). That is why the architects try to find a way to construct systems with "mixed" features.

An example is the CM-5 system [45] which is basically a MIMD system: each node PE can execute independently its own program stored in its local instruction memory. At the same time, the hardware support of global synchronization (the so-called *barrier synchronization*) is provided, allowing us to retain all the advantages of the data parallel style typical of SIMD systems.

Recently, wide interest was attracted by *Heterogeneous Computing,* which implies a *distributed* system of several *commercially available computers* of diverse architectures. In such an environment, the user is able to vary flexibly the style of programming, in accordance with the characteristics of his problems.

Heterogeneous computing is defined as a "coordinated effective use of diverse high-performance machines (including parallel machines) to provide fast processing for computationally demanding tasks that have diverse computing needs" [56].

The Combined Architecture clearly represents a different approach to Heterogeneous Computing. In combined architectures one deals with *concentrated* systems, in which various styles of programming are supported by appropriate *specialized hardware modules.* The proper selection of the assortment of these modules is of vital importance for efficient implementation of the combined architecture systems. The types and the number of functional modules have been briefly discussed above (see Section 8.3.1). From the viewpoint of organization of the heterogeneous environment in combined architecture, it will be useful to introduce the notion of *processing type.*

This notion is heuristic, and we do not attempt here to prove its functional completeness nor its other abstract characteristics. The single purpose of our analysis is to provide high performance of the system, and to make a well-founded selection of the set of hardware modules.

The initial point of this classification is the study of the features of massive operations used in existing computing systems and programming languages (see, for instance, [51]). As mentioned in the Preface, there exist three large groups of processing types requiring, for their efficient execution, different structures of hardware. These are:

A. The proper calculations (arithmetical processing);

B. Non-numerical processing;

C. Transformation of data structures.

In group A, the following processing types can be distinguished: component-wise computations with integer, real, or complex arrays, where the arguments and the result have equal dimensionalities; and the reductive computations with integer, real, or complex arrays, where the result is a scalar.

The main processing types of the group B are: data retrieval (simple and complex associative searches); set-theoretical operations; special operations of relational algebra; and some other operations pertaining to artificial intelligence problems.

The most used processing types of the group C are: compression; expansion; transposition; broadcasting; masking; sorting. It should be noted that processing in the group C transforms the structure of data arrays but does not change the values of the elements.

The processing type is, essentially, a hardware procedure chosen from the program. It is supposed that an appropriate specialized device exists, or can be developed, best corresponding to the needs of this procedure. Thus, there is something like a mapping: *processing type → hardware module*, which is, evidently, not uniquely defined. Each of the processing types can be implemented by different hardware modules (possibly with different efficiency). On the other hand, a single hardware module, having properties similar to those of a general purpose processor, can, in principle, realize arbitrary processing types (see also Section 8.3.1).

It can be shown that a moderate number of different hardware modules is sufficient to ensure high performance of combined architecture in solving a broad range of most important problems.

Further development of the combined architecture conception leads to combined *embedded* architectures.

The topological similarity of the operational plane (the set of PEs) of a VPS with specialized cellular structures allows us to propose a superposition of these devices. If the operational plane is endowed with features of some specialized structure, then, evidently, the system is enriched: besides all its standard possibilities, it acquires also all the functional possibilities of the embedded structure. Now, we can apply to the array written in the distributed memory of the operational plane not only the universal algorithms of bit-sequential processing common to existing massively parallel SIMD systems, but also such methods as systolic processing, quasi-analogue processing characteristic for DF-structures, etc. The corresponding procedures can be represented as special microprograms of the VPS controller, and can be called up at various stages of solving the problem.

8.5. VLSI Implementation of DF-structures

We have discussed above various reasons for the assumption that DF-structures can constitute the basis of a universal complex of elements ("building blocks") of improved performance and functionality. Such a complex finds broad application in various computing and control systems.

One of the main advantages of DF-structures is their homogeneity. This property makes them very suitable for realization in modern VLSI circuits. At present, the basic structures of VLSI elements are the gate arrays consisting of a large number of "blanks" (transistor cells), placed regularly on the chip. These cells are connected into the required circuit by means of one or several metal layers, or by programming of the internal control storage. The packaging density of millions of gates per chip, and the clock frequency of hundreds of MHz are now typical characteristics for CMOS technology.

Thus, contemporary integrated circuits are ideal for implementation of different homogeneous computing structures. In modern microprocessors, transputers and other computing devices, the register files, adders, multipliers and other circuits of irregular logic structure are formed from the cells of the gate array. In those applications, however, a significant proportion of blanks is often left unused. In cellular arrays and in the DF-structures considered in this book, almost all the chip area can be effectively utilized.

Clearly, the technology is now mature enough for broad application of cellular computing structures. The architecture and circuit engineering, and the "ideology" of operational unit design are now, in a sense, behind the technology. In industry, VLSI chips are widely used to manufacture various memory chips and microprocessors. But what are the future prospects ?

The known term *definition of VLSI* means the functional invention of a design and its agreement with the possibilities of technology. Many companies are now seeking new practicable definitions of their VLSI products.

DF-structures are a possible version of VLSI definition. It could be said that several specialized DF-structures, or maybe one, combined, having an enlarged set of basic operations, can be claimed as a new product, which might be called a *cellular microprocessor.*

Unlike other approaches, the solution of problems is not confined here to application of classical methods of the theory of automata. They are solved, as a rule, in more immediate ways, by means of quasi-analogue simulation of massive parallel functions, and therefore should be more efficient.

In designing new high-performance computing systems, cellular microprocessors can successfully complement existing standard products of the computer industry: RAMs, ROMs, microprocessors, transputers.

The first DF-structure suggested by the author in 1971 [24] was the α-structure (extremum searches). Later on, other DF-structures were designed, and in 1976 a book (in Russian) was published in Novosibirsk [23], summarizing the preliminary results concerning these structures.

Around the same time Kautz, from Stanford Research Institute, studied specialized cellular arrays, though with other features and from another viewpoint [53,54]. In 1978 Ramamoorthy, Turner and Wah published a paper [65] describing cellular arrays implementing equality search, threshold searches and extremum searches.

Some questions concerning the design of cellular arrays were touched on in a short correspondence [49] between the author of this book and the authors of the paper [65].

Later, Davis and Lee [17], as well as Feng [22], made some interesting investigations improving the time estimations of basic searches compared with the results mentioned above.

The distinguishing features of the DF-structures considered in this book are the broad set of basic functions and the flexible functional behaviour, unlike other cellular structures described in the literature.

Some DF-structures (particularly α and λ) allow organization of various modes of data processing, not following directly from their basic operations. Examples of such unusual approaches were given in Chapters 4 to 8. This flexibility, together with high level of parallelism and perfect conformity to VLSI technology, may eventually be a decisive factor for the practical use of DF-structures in future computing systems.

References

1. Akushsky I.Y. and Yuditzky D.I. *Computer arithmetic in residue number systems.* Moscow: Soviet Radio, 1968. (In Russian).
2. Anishev P.A., et al. *Parallel microprogramming methods.* Novosibirsk: Nauka, 1981. (In Russian).
3. Barnes G.H., et al. The ILLIAC IV computer. *IEEE Transactions on Computers,* 1968, Vol.C-17, No.8, pp.746-757.
4. Baron R.J. and Higbie L.C. *Computer Architecture: Case Studies.* Reading, Mass.: Addison-Wesley, 1992.
5. Batcher K.E. Design of a Massively Parallel Processor. *IEEE Transactions on Computers,* 1980, Vol.C-29, No.9, pp.836-844.
6. Batcher K.E. Sorting networks and their applications. -In: *AFIPS Confer. Proc., 1968 SJCC,* Vol.32, pp.307-314.
7. Bertin P., Roncin D., and Vuillemin J. *Introduction to programmable active memories.* DEC Paris Res. Lab., June 1989. Report No.3.
8. Blelloch G.E. *Vector Models for Data-Parallel Computing.* Cambridge, Mass.: MIT Press, 1990.
9. Blewins D.W., et al. BLITZEN: a highly integrated massively parallel machine. *J. Parallel Distrib. Comput.,* 1990, Vol.8, No.2, pp.150-160.
10. Boghosian B.M. Computational physics on the Connection Machine. *Computers in Physics,* Vol.4, No.1, 1990.
11. Boral H. and Redfield S. Database machine morphology. -In: *Proc. Intern. Confer. on VLDB,* Stockholm, 1985, pp.59-71.
12. Broomel G. and Heath J.R. Classification categories and historical development of circuit switching topologies. *ACM Computing Surveys,* 1983, Vol.15, No.2, pp.95-133.
13. *CHS 2x4 custom computer.* User manual. Edinburgh: Algotronix, Ltd, 1990.
14. Codd E.F. A relational model of large shared data banks. *Comm. ACM,* 1970, Vol.13, No.6, pp.377-387.
15. Codd E.F. *Cellular Automata.* New York: Academic Press, 1968.
16. *Computing and Control,* 1991, Vol.2, No.3, p.102.

180

17. Davis W.A. and Lee D.-L. Fast search algorithms for associative memories. *IEEE Transactions on Computers,* 1986, Vol.C-35, No.5, pp.456-461.
18. Demos G. Issues in applying massively parallel computing power. *Supercomputing Applications,* 1990, Vol.4, No.4, pp.90-105.
19. Duncan R. Parallel computer architectures. -In: *Advances in Computers,* Academic Press, 1992, Vol.34, pp.113-157.
20. Faddeeva V.N. and Gavurin M.K. *Bessel functions $J_n(x)$ of integer indexes from 0 to 120.* (L.V.Kantorovich, ed.). Moscow, 1950 (In Russian).
21. Feng T.-Y. Data manipulating functions in parallel processors and their implementations. *IEEE Transactions on Computers,* 1974, Vol.C-23, No.3, pp.309-318.
22. Feng T.-Y. Search algorithms for bis-sequential machines. *Journ. Parallel Distrib. Comput.,* 1990, Vol.8, No.1, pp.1-9.
23. Fet Ya.I. *Bulk information processing in specialized cellular processors.* Novosibirsk: Nauka, 1976. (In Russian).
24. Fet Ya.I. Data sorting device. *USSR Inventors Certificate No.424141,* Cl.G 06F 7/00, 1971. (In Russian).
25. Fet Ya.I. Massively parallel systems of combined architecture. -In: *Mitteilungen GI "Parallel Algoritmen und Rechenstrukturen",* Dresden, 1993,Vol.12, pp.285-298.
26. Fet Ya.I. *Parallel Processors in Control Systems.* Moscow: Energoizdat, 1981. (In Russian).
27. Flynn M.J. Very high-speed computing systems. *Proc. IEEE,* 1966, Vol.54, No.12, pp.1901-1906.
28. Foster C.C. *Content addressable parallel processors.* New York: Van Nostrand Reinhold, 1976.
29. Fuller R.H. and Estrin G. Some applications for content-addressable memories. *AFIPS Confer. Proc., 1963 FJCC,* Vol.24, pp.495-508.
30. Gardner P.L. Functional memory and its microprogramming implementations. *IEEE Transactions on Computers,* 1971, Vol.C-20, No.7, pp.764-775.
31. Haendler W. Dynamic computer structures for manifold utilization. *Parallel Computing,* 1985, Vol.2, pp.15-32.
32. Haendler W. *History of computers - a taxonomic approach.* Novosibirsk, 1992.
33. Haendler W. Nature needed billions of years... -In: *Proc. of the Intern. Confer. "Parallel Comp. Technol." (N.N.Mirenkov, ed.).* Singapore: World Scientific, 1991, pp.1-16.
34. Haendler W. On classification schemes for computers in the post-von-Neumann era. *Lect. Notes in Computer Science.* Berlin: Springer, 1975, Vol.24, pp.439-452.
35. Haendler W. and Fet Ya.I. Vertical processing in parallel computing systems. -In: *Proc. of the Intern. Confer."Parallel Comp. Technol."* (N.N.Mirenkov, ed.). Singapore: World Scientific, 1991, pp.56-75.
36. Hardgrave W.T., Sibley E.H., Kogalovsky M.R., Kogutovsky V.V. Problems of positional and integer set processor implementation. -In: *"Data Models and Database Systems. Proc. of the Joint US-USSR Seminar".* Austin, Texas, Oct.25-27, 1979, pp.123-143.

181

37. Hawthorn P.B. Is there an ideal database machine? -In: *Proc. COMCON Spring 1981 CSIC*, pp.104-107.
38. Hawthorn P.B. and DeWitt D.J. Performance analysis of alternative database machines architectures. *IEEE Transactions on Software Engineering*, 1982, Vol.SE-8, No.1, pp.61-75.
39. Hennessy J.L. and Patterson D.A. *Computer Architecture: A Quantitative Approach*. Morgan-Kaufmann. 1990.
40. Hennie F.C. *Finite-state models for logical machines*. New York-London-Sydney: Wiley, 1968.
41. Hennie F.C. *Iterative arrays of logical circuits*. Cambridge, Mass.: MIT Press, 1961.
42. *High-Performance Computing Review*. 1994 Annual Vendor Guide. Austin, TX: Publ. and Comm. Inc., 1994.
43. Hillis W.D. Co-evolving parasites improve simulation evolution as an optimization procedure. *Physica D*, 1990, Vol.42, pp.228-234.
44. Hillis W.D. The Connection Machine: a computer architecture based on cellular automata. *Physica D*, 1984, Vol.10, pp.213-228.
45. Hillis W.D. and Tucker L.W. Connection Machine: a scalable supercomputer. *Comm. ACM.*, 1993, Vol.36, No.11, pp.31-40.
46. Hord R.M. *Parallel Supercomputing in SIMD Architecrures*. Boca Raton: CRC Press, 1990.
47. Hsiao D.K. (ed.) *Advanced database machine architecture*. Prentice-Hall, 1983.
48. *IDM-500 product description*. Britton-Lee, Inc., 1980.
49. *IEEE Transactions on Computers*, 1980, Vol.C-29, No.8.
50. Il'in V.P. and Fet Ya.I. Grid massively parallel processor. *Proc. of the 5th Intern. PARLE Confer. (A.Bode et.al., eds.)*. Berlin: Springer Verlag, 1993, pp. 752-755. (LNCS, Vol.694).
51. Iverson K.E. *A programming language*. New York-London: Wiley, 1962.
52. Kapustyan V.M., Belyaev I.P., and Medvedev B.G. Combinatorial memory. *Trans. USSR Acad. Sci. on Techn. Cybern.*, 1980, No.2, pp.114-127. (In Russian).
53. Kautz W.H. An augmented content-addressed memory array for implementation with large-scale integration. *Journ. of the ACM*, 1971, Vol.18, No.1, pp.19-33.
54. Kautz W.H. Cellular logic-in-memory arrays. *IEEE Transactions on Computers*, 1969, Vol.C-18, No.8, pp.719-727.
55. Kautz W.H., et al. Cellular interconnection arrays. *IEEE Trans. on Computers*, 1968, Vol.C-17, No.5, pp.443-451.
56. Khokhar A.A., et al. Heterogeneous Computing: challenges and opportunities. *Computer*, 1993, Vol.26, No.6, pp.18-27.
57. Knuth D. *The Art of Computer Programming. Vol.3, Sorting and Searching*. New York: Addison-Wesley, 1973.
58. Lawrie D.H. Access and alignment of data in array processors. *IEEE Transactions on Computers*, 1975, Vol.C-24, No.12, pp.1145-1155.
59. Leighton F.T. *Introduction to Parallel Algorithms and Architectures: Arrays, Trees, Hypercubes*. Palo Alto, CA: Morgan-Kaufmann, 1992.
60. Levin M.H. Retrieval of ordered lists from a content-addressed memory. *RCA Review*, 1962, Vol.23, No2, pp.215-229.
61. *Microprocessors and Microsystems*, 1990, Vol.14, No.2.
62. Ozkarahan E. *Database machines and database management*. Englewood Cliffs: Prentice-Hall, 1986.

63. Parker D.S. Notes on shuffle-exchange type switching networks. *IEEE Transactions on Computers*, 1980, Vol.C-29, No.2, pp.213-222.
64. Pease M.C. Matrix inversion using parallel processing. *Journ. of the ACM*, 1967, Vol.14, No.4, pp.757-764.
65. Ramamoorthy C.V., Turner J.L., and Wah B.W. A design of a fast cellular associative memory for ordered retrieval. *IEEE Trans. on Computers*, 1978, Vol.C-27, No.10, pp.800-815.
66. Reddaway S.F. DAP - a distributed array processor. *1-st Annual Simp. on Computer Architecture (IEEE/ACM)*, Florida, 1982.
67. Rudolph J.A. A production implementation of an associative array processor - STARAN. *AFIPS Confer. Proc., 1972 FJCC*. Vol.41, Pt.1, pp.229-241.
68. Schneck P.B. Supercomputers. -In: *Annu. Rev. Comp. Sci.*, 1990, Vol.4, pp.13-36.
69. Sedukhin S.G. Design and analysis of systolic algorithms for the algebraic path problem. *Computers and Artificial Intelligence*. 1992, Vol.11, No.3, pp.269-292.
70. Shibayama S., at al. A relational database machine with large semiconductor disk and hardware relational algebra processor. *New Generation Computing*, 1984, Vol.2, No.2, pp.131-155.
71. Slade A.E. and MacMahon H.C. A cryotron catalog memory. *AFIPS Confer. Proc., 1956 EJCC*, Vol.10, pp. 115-120.
72. Slotnick D.L. Logic-per-track devices. *Advances in Computers*. New York: Academic Press, 1970, Vol.10, pp.291-296.
73. Slotnick D.L., et al. The SOLOMON computer. *AFIPS Confer. Proc. 1962 FJCC*, Vol.22, pp.97-107.
74. Stone H.S. Parallel processing with the perfect shuffle. *IEEE Transactions on Computers*, 1971, Vol.C-20, No.2, pp.153-161.
75. Suvorov E.V. and Fet Ya.I. Database processors. *Soviet Journ. of Comput. and Syst. Sci.*, 1986, No.2, pp.120-130.
76. Toffoly T. and Margolus N. *Cellular automata machines: a new environment for modeling*. Cambridge, Mass.: MIT Press, 1987.
77. Trew A. and Wilson G. (Eds.) *Past, Present, Parallel: A Survey of Available Parallel Computer Systems*. London-Berlin-Heidelberg: Springer-Verlag, 1991.
78. Tucker L.W. and Robertson G.G. Architecture and applications of the Connection Machine. *IEEE Computer*, 1988, Vol.21, No.8, pp.26-38.
79. Unger S.H. A computer oriented toward spatial problems. *Proc.IRE*, 1958, Vol.46, No.10, pp.1744-1750.
80. Vazhenin A.P., Sedukhin S.G., and Fet Ya.I. High-performance computing systems of combined architecture. *-In: Proc of the Intern. Confer. "Parallel Computing Technologies"* (*N.N.Mirenkov, ed.*), Singapore: World Scientific, 1991, pp.246-257.
81. Wilson K.G. Grand challenges to computational science. *Future Generation Computer Systems*, 1989, Vol.5, No.2-3, pp.171-189.
82. Wu C. and Feng T.-Y. Universality of the shuffle-exchange network. *IEEE Transactions on Computers*, 1981, Vol.C-30, No. 5, pp. 324-331.
83. Yevreinov E.V. and Kosarev Yu.G. *High-performance homogeneous universal computing systems*. Novosibirsk: Nauka, 1966. (In Russian).

List of Acronyms

AA   Adder-Accumulator
AAP   Associative Array Processor
ALU   Arithmetic-Logic Unit
BLM   Binary Label Matrix
BLV   Binary Label Vector
CAM   Content-Addressed Memory
CAT   Combinatorial Attribute Tree
CM   Connection Machine
CT   Code Transformer
CU   Control Unit
CVR   Control Vector Register
DAP   Distributed Array Processor
DBA   Database Accelerator
DBM   Database Machine
DBMS   Database Management System
DC   Digital Compressor
DF-structure   Distributed Functional structure
DFN   Disjunctive Normal Form
DST   Data Structure Transformation
ECS   Erlangen Classification Scheme
EM   Elementary Machine
FIFO   First In First Out
FM   Functional Memory

GMPP   Grid Massively Parallel Processor
HCM   Homogeneous Computing Media
ICN   Interconnection Network
LAM   Labelled Array Method
LBS   Logical Bit String
LCA   Logic Cell Array
LIM   Local Interconnection Module
LOS   Leading Ones Selector
MIMD   Multiple Instruction Multiple Data
MISD   Multiple Instruction Single Data
MPP   Massively Parallel Processor
OU   Operational Unit
PAB   Programmable Active Bit
PAM   Programmable Active Memory
PDNF   Principal Disjunctive Normal Form
PE   Processing Element
PLA   Programmable Logic Array
RAM   Random Access Memory
RAP   Relational Associative Processor
RC   Residue Calculator
RNS   Residue Number System
ROM   Read Only Memory
SIMD   Single Instruction Multiple Data
SISD   Single Instruction Single Data
SIP   Set Intersection Processor
SSM   Standard Stencil Memory
SSR   Standard Stencil Register
TFM   Table look-up Functional Module
UC   Unitary Code
UCD   Unitary-Coded Decimal
UCS   Universal (parallel) Computing System
UPC   Unit Positional Code
VLSI   Very Large Scale Integration
VPS   Vertical Processing System

Author Index

Babbage Ch. 7
Batcher K.E. 144-147,152
Boral H. 109
Codd E.F. 30,106
Davis W.A. 178
Estrin G. 34
Feng T.-Y. 141,144,151,178
Flynn M.J. 9,107
Foster C.C. 36
Fuller R.H. 34
Gardner P.L. 64
Haendler W. 9,12,107,164
Hardgrave W.T. 120
Hawthorn P.B. 114
Hennie F.C. 16,22,24
Hillis W.D. 15
Hsiao D.K. 107,108,110
Iverson K.E. 151
Kantorovich L.V. 7
Kapustyan V.M. 124
Kautz W.H. 141,178
Knuth D.E. 144
Lawrie D.H. 134

Lee D.-L. 178
Levin M.H. 147
Margolus N. 27
McMahon H.C. 31
von Neumann J. 22,159
Ozkarahan E. 107,114,115
Parker D.S. 140
Pease M.C. 136
Ramamoorthy C.V. 178
Redfield S. 109
Slade A.E. 31
Slotnick D.L. 8,9,106
Stone H.S. 136,139
Suvorov E.V. 115
Toffoly T. 27
Turing A.M. 22
Turner J. 178
Unger S.H. 7
Wah B.W. 178
Wilson K.G. 1
Wu C. 141,144
Yevreinov E.V. 8-9,27

Subject Index

Accelerator *171*
  database accelerator (DBA) *110*
Adder
  binary adder *19-21*
    parallel binary adder *21*
    sequential binary adder *20*
  decimal adder *87*
  (mod m) adder *94-100*
    homogeneous (mod m) adder *95-98*
    universal (mod m) adder *96*
  vertical adder *80-82*
Adjacency
  matrix *55-57*
  search *44-46*
Aggregate function(s) *112,128-129*
Algebra, relational *106,112-113,115,120,175*
AND gate *28,29,89-90*
AND matrix *63-64,66*
Architecture
  combined architecture *170-172,174-176*
Arithmetic unit *7,91,94*
Arithmetic-logic unit *10,171*
Array
  programmable logic array (PLA) *63-65*
  systolic array *10,170*
Associative
  array processor *106*
  memory *31-33,35-36,60-62*
  search *33,35,106*
  tag *31,36*
Atomic permutation *152*
Automaton *18-24*

Back-end processor
   hardware back-end processor   *108*
   software back-end processor   *109*
Batcher's network   *144-147*
Between-the-limits search   *43*
Binary adder   *19-21*
   parallel binary adder   *21*
   sequential binary adder   *20*
Binary label vector (BLV)   *115-120*
Binary label matrix (BLM)   *129-130*
BLITZEN   *12,14*
Building block   *163*
Butterfly   *137,139*

Calculus, relational   *106*
CAM (content-addressed memory)   *31-33,35-36,60-62*
Cell   *22,24,27*
   E-cell   *134-135,137,153*
Cellular Automata Machine   *27*
Centralized control   *133*
Channel
   control channel   *132*
   input data channel   *132*
   output data channel   *132*
Characteristic vector   *136-137*
Classification   *47*
   Erlangen classification scheme   *10-11,13*
   Flinn's classification   *10*
CM (Connection Machine)   *12-14,174*
Code
   unit positional code (UPC)   *68*
   unitary code (UC)   *67*
      compressed unitary code (CUC)   *67*
      normalized unitary code (NUC)   *67*
      code transformer   *74*
Coder   *86*
   residue coder   *101*
Combinational circuit   *20,28*
Combinatorial attribute tree (CAT)   *125*
Combinatorial memory   *124-127*
Commutator   *33*
   flat commutator   *140*
Comparand   *33,37,130*
Comparand register   *33*
Comparator   *144-145*
   parallel comparator   *167*
Comparison, component-wise   *46,128*
Compressed unitary code (CUC)   *67*
Compressing permutation   *157*
Compression   *48-50,151*
Compressor   *68*
   digital   *68*
   logarithmic   *73*
   pipelined   *71*

Computation
  parallel   5
  quasi-analogue   *169-170,176*
Computer
  non-numerical   *107,114,127*
  von Neumann's   *10,22,159*
Computing
  heterogeneous computing   *173-174*
  homogeneous computing media (HCM)   *8-9,27-29,53*
Configuration   *24-25*
Concentrator   *132*
Connection
  nearest neighbour   *8,12*
Connection Machine (CM)   *12-14,174*
Connector   *132*
  blocking   *133*
  non-blocking   *133,154*
  rearrangeable   *133*
Content-addressed memory (CAM)   *31-33,35-36,60-62*
Control
  centralized control   *133*
  control channel   *132*
  distributed control   *133*
Controller
  intelligent controller   *108,110*
Copying   *151*
Coprocessor   *170*
Crossbar switch   *133-134*
Cyclic shift   *95,153*

DAP (distributed array processor)   *8,14*
Data
  database   *104-120*
    database accelerator (DBA)   *110*
    database machine (DBM)   *106-115*
    database management system (DBMS)   *108*
    relational database   *106,120*
    relational database engine   *113*
  data parallel programming   *15*
  data structure transformation (DST)   *150,175*
  data retrieval   *104,147*
Decimal
  adder   *87*
  multiplier   *89*
Decoder   *87*
Descending ordering   *144*
Destination tag   *135*
Digital
  compressor   *68*
    logarithmic   *73*
    pipelined   *71*

Disjunctive
  normal form   *58-60*
  reading   *52*
Distributed control   *133,139*
Distributed functional structures (DF-structures)   *29-79*
  α-structure   *37-40,51-66,154-156*
  β-structure   *40-41*
  γ-structure   *43-44*
  ε-structure   *41-43*
  υ-structure   *44-46*
  η-structure   *46-47*
  λ-structure   *48-50,67-79,156-158*
  ρ-structure   *47-48*
  ω-structure   *129-130*
Distributed processing   *16*
Duplication   *52*

Element
  2α-element   *61*
  $\rho\alpha$-element   *60*
  processing element (PE)   *7,10,12-15,165-166*
  threshold element   *78-79*
Embedding   *27-28,176*
Entry vector   *117*
Equality search   *36*
Equivalence function   *31*
Erlangen classification scheme   *10-11,13*
Expander   *133*
Expanding permutation   *159*
Expansion   *151*

Fine-grained system   *11*
Finite automaton   *18-19,22,24*
Flip
  network   *152-154*
  permutation(s)   *152-154*
Function
  aggregate function   *112,128-129*
  equivalence function   *31*
  logical function   *58-60*
Functional memory   *64-66*

Gates
  AND   *28,29,89-90*
  NOT   *54*
  OR   *28-29,90*
  XOR   *65-66,91*
Granularity   *11*
Grid massively parallel processor (GMPP)   *164-167*

Hardware back-end   *108-109*
Hierarchical memory subsystem   *113*
High-performance computing system   *1-2,14,173-176*

Homogeneous
  computing media (HCM)   *8-9,27-29,53*
  (mod m) adder   *95-98*
Horizontal processing   *16*

Identifier
  element identifier   *120*
  positional identifier   *120-121*
  tuple identifier   *113*
ILLIAC IV   *9,10*
Inequality search   *37*
Inner product processor   *82*
Input data channel   *132*
Intelligent controller   *108,110*
Interconnection element(s)   *56-58*
  "CONNECTION"   *28,56,58*
  "ISOLATE"   *56,57*
  "NOT"   *56,57*
  "TRANSFER"   *28,55*
Interconnection network (ICN)   *12,13,131-134,141,154,165*
Internal memory   *19*
Interpolation   *85,166*
Interval   *83-84*
Iterative network   *22-24*

Label
  binary label matrix (BLM)   *129-130*
  binary label vector (BLV)   *115-120*
Labelled array method (LAM)   *115-120*
Large-grained system   *11*
Leading one's selector (LOS)   *80-81*
Levin's method   *147*
Logarithmic digital compressor   *73*
Logic
  logic cell array (LCA)   *30*
  logical bit string (LBS)   *122*
  programmable logic array (PLA)   *63-65*
Look-up
  table look-up   *83,85,166*

Machine
  Cellular Automata Machine   *27*
  Connection Machine (CM)   *12-14,174*
  database machine (DBM)   *106-115*
    CAFS   *106*
    CASSM   *106*
    DBC   *106*
    Delta   *111-115*
    IDM-500   *110-111*
    RAP   *115*
    RARES   *106*

Masking *151*
Massive parallel processor (MPP) *8,12-14*
Matrix
  adjacency matrix *55-57*
  AND-matrix *63-64,66*
  binary label matrix (BLM) *129-130*
  OR-matrix *63-64*
Maximum search *37*
Media
  homogeneous computing media (HCM) *8-9,27-29,53*
Memory *51-53*
  combinatorial memory *124-127*
  content-addressed memory (CAM) *31-33,35-36,60-62*
  functional memory *64-66*
  hierarchical memory subsystem *113*
  internal memory *19*
  local memory *12*
  Programmable Active Memory (PAM) *30*
  table memory *83-85*
Microprocessor *177*
  cellular microprocessor *177*
MIMD-system *9*
Minimum search *40-41*
Mirror permutation *138*
(mod m) adder *94-100*
  homogeneous (mod m) adder *95-98*
Morphological description *109*
MPP (massive parallel processor) *8,12-14*
Multiplication table *89,103*
Multiplier
  decimal multiplier *89*
  vertical multiplier *81-82*

Neighbour
  nearest neighbour connection *8,12*
Network
  Batcher's network *144-147*
  flip network *152-154*
  interconnection network (ICN) *12,13,131-134,141,154,165*
    universal interconnection network *144*
  iterative network *22-24*
  shuffle-exchange network *137*
  sorting network *144*
  Stone's network *136,139*
  Ω-network *139-141*
von Neumann computer *10,22,159*
Non-numerical
  computer *107,114*
  problem(s) *104*
  processing *115*
  processor *106*
Normalized unitary code (NUC) *67*

Operation(s)
  ordering operation *116*
    ascending *116,144,149*
    descending *144*
  set-theoretical operation(s) *104,129,175*
  special operations of LAM *118-119*
OR
  OR gate *28-29,90*
  OR-matrix *63-64,66*
Ordered retrieval *148*
Output data channel *132*

Parallel
  binary adder *21*
  comparator *167*
  software primitives *15*
  substitution system *24-26*
  variable *15*
Parallelism
  fine-grained *14*
  large-grained *14*
PE (processing element) *7,10,12-15,165-166*
Perfect shuffle *136*
Performance
  peak performance *2*
  real performance *173*
Permutation
  atomic permutation *152*
  compressing permutation *157*
  expanding permutation *159*
  flip permutation *152-154*
  permutation vector *135,167*
  shift permutation *153*
PLA (programmable logic array) *63-65*
Placing *151*
Polyadic number system *125-127*
Positional
  positional set *120-124*
  unit positional code (UPC) *68*
Processing
  associative processing *171*
  distributed processing *16*
  horizontal processing *16*
  non-numerical processing *102-104,171*
  numerical processing *171*
  pipelined-stream processing *111*
  processing element (PE) *6,10-12,166*
  processing type *174-175*
  vertical processing *16*
    vertical processing system (VPS) *12-15,171-172*

Processor
  associative array processor   *106*
  back-end processor   *108-109*
  inner product processor   *82*
  non-numerical processor   *106*
  set-intersection processor (SIP)   *129-130*
Programmable logic array (PLA)   *63-65*
Programming style   *16,174*

Quasi-analogue
  computation   *169-170,176*
  processing   *159,176*
  simulation   *33*
Quasi-associative processing   *36,107,128*

RAM   *52,177*
Register
  comparand register   *33*
Relational
  algebra   *106,112-113,115,120,175*
  calculus   *106*
  database   *106,112,120*
  database engine   *112*
  model   *106*
Residue   *91*
  partial residue   *100*
  residue calculator   *99*
  residue coder   *101*
Residue number system (RNS)   *91-93*
Retrieval
  data retrieval   *104,147*
  ordered retrieval   *148*
Robot control   *162*
ROM   *177*

Scanning   *15*
Scheme
  Erlangen classification scheme   *10-13*
Search
  adjacency search   *44-46*
  associative search   *33,35,106*
  between-the-limits search   *43*
  equality search   *36*
  inequality search   *37*
  maximum search   *37*
  minimum search   *40-41*
  threshold search   *37,41-43,128*
Selector
  leading one's selector (LOS)   *80-81*
Separating vector   *116-117*
Sequential binary adder   *20*

Set
    positional set   *120-124*
    Set-Intersection Processor (SIP)   *129-130*
    set-theoretical operation(s)   *104,129,175*
Shuffle
    perfect shuffle   *136*
Simulation
    quasi-analogue simulation   *33*
SIP (Set Intersection Processor)   *129-130*
SOLOMON   *7-8*
Sorting network   *144*
Space-time transformation   *16*
Special operations of LAM   *118,119*
Spreading   *15*
STARAN   *12-14,115*
Stone's network   *136,139*
Subinterval   *83-84*
Substitution
    parallel substitution system   *24-26*
System
    fine-grained system   *11*
    high-performance computing system   *1-2,14,173-176*
    large-grained system   *11*
    MIMD-system   *9*
    parallel substitution system   *24-26*
    polyadic number system   *125-127*
    residue number system (RNS)   *91-93*
    SIMD-system   *8,10*
    unitary-coded decimal system (UCD-system)   *89-90*
    vertical processing system (VPS)   *12-15,171-172*
Systolic array   *10,170*

Table
    addition table   *88*
    diagonal table of Cauchy-Cantor   *123*
    multiplication table   *89,103*
    table automaton   *83*
    table look-up   *83,85,166*
    table memory   *83-85*
    truth table   *19-20,96*
    value table   *123*
Tag
    associative tag   *31,36*
    destination tag   *135*
Threshold
    element   *78-79*
    search   *37,41-43,128*
Transformation
    data structure transformation (DST)   *150,175*
    space-time transformations   *16*

Transformer
  BCD→UPC   *86-87*
  NUC→UPC   *76-77*
  UC→NUC   *74*
  UPC→NUC   *78*
  UPC→2   *74*
  2→NUC   *74-77*
  2→RNS   *99,101*
  2→UC   *74*
  2→UPC   *74*
  10→BCD   *86*
Transposition   *105*
Transputer   *177*
Triplet   *10-11*
Truth table   *19-20,96*
Tuple identifier   *113*

UC (unitary code)   *67*
UCD (unitary-coded decimal system)   *89-90*
Unit
  arithmetic-logic unit   *10,171*
  arithmetic unit   *7,91,94*
Unit positional code (UPC)   *68*
Unitary code (UC)   *67*
  compressed unitary code (CUC)   *67*
  normalized unitary code (NUC)   *67*

Value table   *123*
Vector
  binary label vector (BLV)   *115-120*
  characteristic vector   *136-137*
  entry vector   *117*
  permutation vector   *135,167*
  separating vector   *116-117*
Vertical
  adder   *80-82*
  addition   *80-81*
  multiplier   *81-82*
  processing   *16*
Vertical processing system (VPS)   *12-15,171-172*
VLSI   *36,176-177*
Von Neumann's computer   *10,22,159*

Weighting   *67*
Workstation   *11*